UNDERSTANDING CORONA VIRUSES

SARS, MERS, AND THE COVID-19 PANDEMIC

CONNIE GOLDSMITH

TWENTY-FIRST CENTURY BOOKS / MINNEAPOLIS

THIS BOOK IS DEDICATED TO THE HEALTH-CARE WORKERS AND FIRST RESPONDERS WHO RISKED THEIR LIVES TO SAVE OTHERS DURING THE SARS-COV-2 PANDEMIC.

Twenty-First Century Books™
An imprint of Lerner Publishing Group, Inc.
241 First Avenue North
Minneapolis, MN 55401 USA

For reading levels and more information, look up this title at www.lernerbooks.com.

Main body text set in Adobe Garamond Pro.
Typeface provided by Adobe Systems.

Library of Congress Cataloging-in-Publication Data

Names: Goldsmith, Connie, 1945– author.
Title: Understanding coronaviruses : SARS, MERS, and the COVID-19 pandemic / Connie Goldsmith.
Description: Minneapolis : Twenty-First Century Books , [2022] | Includes bibliographical references and index. | Audience: Ages 13–18 | Audience: Grades 7–9 | Summary: "While many scientists believed influenza would cause the next pandemic, no one was prepared for the new strain of coronavirus that appeared in 2019. Understanding Coronaviruses examines SARS-CoV-2, its origin, its impact on daily life, and how COVID-19 compares to coronavirus diseases"— Provided by publisher.
Identifiers: LCCN 2021058770 (print) | LCCN 2021058771 (ebook) | ISBN 9781728428888 (library binding) | ISBN 9781728430935 (ebook)
Subjects: LCSH: COVID-19 (Disease)—Juvenile literature. | Coronavirus infection—Juvenile literature.
Classification: LCC RA644.C67 G648 2022 (print) | LCC RA644.C67 (ebook) | DDC 362.1962/414—dc23

LC record available at https://lccn.loc.gov/2021058770
LC ebook record available at https://lccn.loc.gov/2021058771

Manufactured in the United States of America
1-49410-49508-4/12/2021

CONTENTS

CHAPTER 1
THE HERO DOCTOR'S WARNING 4

CHAPTER 2
MEET THE MICROBES. 10

CHAPTER 3
MEET THE CORONAVIRUSES 24

CHAPTER 4
GOING VIRAL. 34

CHAPTER 5
SCHOOL'S OUT! 50

CHAPTER 6
FLATTENING THE CURVE 60

CHAPTER 7
HEALTH CARE FIGHTS BACK 74

CHAPTER 8
THE WINTER SURGE 96

CHAPTER 9
FINDING A NEW NORMAL 110

GLOSSARY. 120
SOURCE NOTES 122
SELECTED BIBLIOGRAPHY 132
FURTHER INFORMATION 136
INDEX 142

THE HERO DOCTOR'S WARNING

Dr. Li Wenliang studied medicine at Wuhan University in Wuhan, a large city of about eleven million people along the Yangtze River in central China. After medical school, he went to work as an eye doctor in Wuhan Central Hospital in 2014. In December 2019, Li noticed a cluster of patients with respiratory symptoms similar to severe acute respiratory syndrome (SARS). SARS emerged in 2002, making it the first new disease of the twenty-first century. The seven patients were quarantined in Li's hospital. Most of them had something in common. They had recently visited a local seafood market.

Li wanted to alert his fellow physicians about the outbreak of a possible SARS-related virus. One patient's lab tests showed the man had been infected by a coronavirus, the type of virus that causes SARS. Li sent a message to his school alumni group using WeChat, a Chinese social network. He advised his friends to avoid infection by wearing protective clothing. "I only wanted to remind my university classmates to

be careful," Li said. He became worried when the posting went viral. "I realized it was out of my control and I would probably be punished."

He was correct.

Four days later, the Wuhan Public Security Bureau summoned Li to its offices and forced him to sign a form that accused him of making false comments and of disturbing the social order. The police threatened he would be "brought to justice" if he did not sign his name to the lie. Li signed. The form, in which he acknowledged that he made false statements and that his behavior had been illegal, circulated online in China.

The Chinese government allowed Li to return to work. A week later, he treated a woman with the eye disease glaucoma. Neither she nor Li knew that she also had the new coronavirus. By January 10, 2020, Li was coughing and had a fever. Two days later, he was in an isolation room at the hospital. Many of the patients he had cared for became ill and were hospitalized. On January 20, China declared the outbreak an emergency.

It was too late for Li, however. His condition continued to worsen, and he died on February 7 at the age of thirty-four in the Wuhan hospital. He left his pregnant wife and his small son behind. Fortunately, they didn't become ill. Across China, people called Li the hero doctor. His colleagues credited him with being the first medical professional to raise concern about the new coronavirus.

Dr. Tom Inglesby, Johns Hopkins Bloomberg School of Public Health in Baltimore, said of Li, "One of the world's most important warning systems for a deadly new outbreak is a doctor's or nurse's recognition that some new disease is emerging and then sounding the alarm. It takes intelligence and courage to step up and say something like that, even in the best of circumstances."

If the government had listened to Li rather than force him to say that he lied, then perhaps the outbreak of the new coronavirus could have been contained, or at least controlled. Perhaps it wouldn't have spread around the world so quickly, becoming a pandemic, killing millions, closing businesses and schools, and upending our way of life.

VISIT TO A WET MARKET

In March 2021, NPR announced that a team from the World Health Organization (WHO) identified the probable source of the new SARS virus. Wildlife farms in China had been breeding exotic animals such as civets, porcupines, and pangolins to sell in wet markets. It's likely the virus spilled over from bats to the animals at those farms. The animals were then sold in the Huanan Seafood Wholesale Market in Wuhan. The crowding in the wet market stressed the animals and weakened their immune systems, giving viruses the chance to mingle and swap genetic material. This can create mutated viruses such as SARS and the new virus that killed Li. These new diseases infect the animals, which then infect humans.

Dr. Linfa Wang was a member of the WHO investigative team that searched for the source of the new virus. He said, "There was massive transmission going on at that [Huanan] market for sure. In the live animal section, they had many positive samples." Chinese authorities shut down the Huanan market on December 31, 2019, and then closed all the wild animal farms that supplied animals to wet markets in February 2020.

Akin to farmers' markets in the United States, Chinese wet markets sell fresh meat and produce. Many also slaughter fish and other live animals, such as civets and pangolins, for their customers. Researchers believe this practice led to the 2002 SARS outbreak and to the outbreak of the new coronavirus as well.

WET MARKET OR MISTAKE AT WUHAN LAB?

In the months after scientists identified the new coronavirus, speculation swirled. Was it really from a wet market? Or was the virus accidentally released from the Wuhan Institute of Virology, a nearby laboratory that studied coronaviruses found in bats? In early May 2020, US president Donald Trump appeared on Fox News and claimed—without evidence, as the *Washington Post* pointed out—that China "made a horrible mistake and didn't want to admit [it]." He said that the virus came from the Wuhan lab, and that he had seen intelligence supporting the lab theory, but that he was "not allowed" to elaborate. "There's a lot of theories," Trump said, "but we have people looking at it very, very strongly. Scientific people, intelligence people, and others."

US secretary of state Mike Pompeo also claimed—also without evidence—that the virus originated in that lab, but he didn't provide any details either. "There's enormous evidence that that's where this [new coronavirus] began," was all Pompeo said on ABC News's *This Week*.

Chinese foreign ministry spokesperson Geng Shuang responded to that claim during a news conference. "The sole purpose for some US politicians trying to fool others with their obvious lies [about the virus's origin] is to shift the blame."

Dr. Ali S. Khan, dean of the University of Nebraska Medical Center, estimates that 70 to 80 percent of emerging infectious diseases reach us through animals or insects. Nearly half of those are viral diseases. The new coronavirus seemed to be no exception.

An article in the *New Yorker* pointed out that only twenty-seven of the earliest forty-one patients had visited the Wuhan market, while the other fourteen had not. Evidence later found that the virus had circulated in Wuhan since November 2019. This suggested that people could have carried the virus *into* the market and could also have carried it *out* of the market, so the market may not have been the source of the virus.

Li Wenliang, depicted in the photo, was the first doctor to identify the new coronavirus and raise the alarm about its potential to turn into a deadly pandemic. After he died from COVID-19 in February 2020, many honored his memory and bravery.

But earlier, in April 2020, NPR corresponded with ten leading scientists who collect and study wild viruses. All ten experts believed the coronavirus was transmitted between animals and humans. "All of the evidence points to this *not* being a laboratory accident," said Jonna Mazet, professor of epidemiology at the University of California, Davis, and head of a global project that monitors emerging diseases.

Many experts had predicted that a new type of influenza was the most likely disease to cause the next global pandemic, but the pandemic that hit the world in 2020 wasn't influenza. Instead, it was the new coronavirus—a distant cousin to SARS and Middle East respiratory syndrome (MERS-CoV)—identified by Li in late 2019. WHO named the virus SARS-CoV-2 for severe acute respiratory syndrome coronavirus 2. The disease it causes is COVID-19, which gets its name because Li first identified it in 2019. SARS-CoV-1 (the updated name for the first identified SARS virus) had higher fatality rates than SARS-CoV-2. But this new coronavirus swept around the globe much more quickly and reached far more countries than any of the others.

And it seemed that no one on the entire planet was immune to it.

MEET THE MICROBES

Microbes are tiny organisms—often called germs—that can only be seen through microscopes. Some benefit us or have no effect on us, while others cause diseases. Bacteria and viruses are the most common microbes that infect humans. Bacteria are one-celled organisms that can live and reproduce by themselves in their environment. For example, if you spill raw chicken juice on the kitchen counter, the bacteria in the juice will live and multiply. Some will even linger after the juice dries up or is wiped up. Different species of bacteria cause strep throat, Lyme disease, tetanus, and sexually transmitted diseases such as gonorrhea and syphilis. Viruses are much simpler than bacteria. They can reproduce only within the living cells of a host organism, such as a human or an animal. Viruses cause influenza, measles, hepatitis, and acquired immunodeficiency syndrome (AIDS).

GETTING TO KNOW BACTERIA

Every human being carries around 3 pounds (1.4 kg) of microscopic bacteria in and on their bodies. While some bacteria can make us very sick or even kill us, most bacteria help us. In fact, we need bacteria. A delicate balance of helpful and dangerous bacteria exists inside the human body. Having the right bacteria in the right places helps to keep us healthy. For example, the bacteria *Streptococcus viridans* lives harmlessly in our noses and throats, crowding out its dangerous cousin, *S. pneumoniae*, which causes pneumonia and meningitis. Bacteria inside our intestines help us digest food. Several kinds of bacteria reside on our skin, where they feast on dead cells. The helpful bacteria we live with stimulate our immune systems to grow stronger, giving us a better chance of resisting harmful bacteria when they show up.

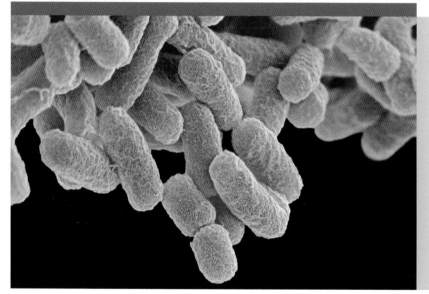

This false-color electron microscope image shows *E. coli*, a type of bacteria that lives in human bodies. Most strains of *E. coli* are harmless, but some can cause food poisoning. When food is contaminated with *E. coli*, manufacturers will issue recalls.

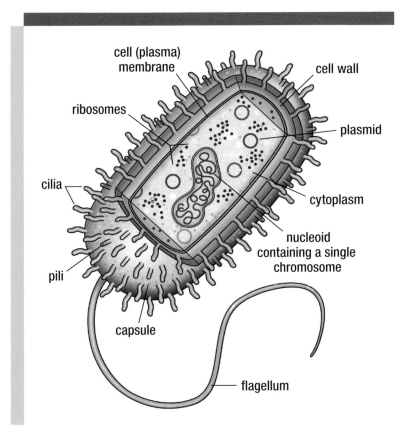

cell (plasma) membrane

cell wall

ribosomes

plasmid

cilia

cytoplasm

pili

nucleoid containing a single chromosome

capsule

flagellum

This diagram illustrates the anatomy of a bacterium.

Many bacteria move with the help of tail-like structures called flagella that propel them through fluids such as blood or water. The flagella help bacteria move toward nutrients and away from toxic substances. Many species of bacteria also have pili, small hairlike structures that help the bacteria attach to other cells such as those that line the inside of a human throat. Pili can transfer genetic information between bacteria by conjugation—when pili from two cells make contact through a bridgelike connection. Conjugation may provide the recipient bacteria with a genetic advantage, such as resistance to a particular antibiotic, that helps it survive and thrive.

Bacteria have cell walls that protect their internal structures. Inside the cell wall is jellylike cytoplasm, which holds the bacteria's inner parts.

- *Ribosomes* take amino acids (organic compounds that combine to form proteins) from the cytoplasm and turn them into proteins using the bacterium's genetic instructions. The cell then uses the proteins to perform various functions.
- *Mitochondria* digest nutrients to provide cells with energy.
- *Chromosomes* hold the genetic information—the deoxyribonucleic acid (DNA) and ribonucleic acid (RNA)—that bacteria need to reproduce. DNA is a substance in every organism's cells that carries genes that control all aspects of the organism's reproduction, appearance, and survival. For example, in humans, genes determine height, eye color, and other physical traits. RNA's main role is to carry instructions from DNA to parts of the cell.
- *Plasmids* are circular strands of DNA that some bacteria carry in their cytoplasm. Bacteria may transfer plasmids to one another through conjugation. The genetic information in plasmids may give a bacterium a genetic advantage.

Bacteria reproduce by dividing into two identical cells. Under the right conditions, some bacteria can divide every twenty to thirty minutes. In eight hours, a single bacterium can produce 16,777,216 bacteria. Bacteria move. They reproduce. They require food to survive, and most require oxygen. They are clearly alive.

VIRUSES: NOT REALLY ALIVE, BUT NOT QUITE DEAD

While bacteria are living organisms, viruses are something else entirely. Not really alive yet not quite dead, viruses are the zombies of the

BUGS ON A PLANE

More than 4.3 billion people traveled by air in 2018, and the number is expected to grow to about 10 billion by 2035. These billions of people bring along more than their suitcases, swimsuits, and snowboards. They also take bacteria and viruses with them. Pathogens—disease-causing microbes—don't possess wings or legs. Instead, they must hitch a ride to reach their final destination. Often that ride is with a passenger sitting for hours inside a crowded plane.

The prolonged close contact during air travel greatly increases the risk of one person passing a pathogen to others. Imagine that you're sitting in the middle row on a flight from San Francisco to New York. It's bad enough to catch a cold from the person seated to your right who coughs all the way. But what's really scary is the possibility that the person to your left is carrying a bad bug without even knowing it. Many diseases can be spread during their incubation period, the time between when a person is infected and when symptoms begin. This means sick people may not yet realize they are sick. Air travel often includes stops and layovers along the way. Each of those layovers and flight changes expose passengers to more people and increases the chance that a passenger will pick up an infection.

Many airlines modified the air circulation systems on their aircraft during the pandemic to decrease the risk of exposure to the coronavirus.

microscopic world. Viruses can't carry out any of the activities that define life. They can't move or reproduce by themselves. Viruses don't need food or oxygen to live. All they need is a living host cell. Without those living cells, viruses lose their ability to reproduce and cause disease. For example, if you have a cold and leave a soiled tissue on the kitchen counter, the viruses in the mucus on the tissue cannot live for more than a few hours and cannot multiply.

Viruses are much smaller than bacteria. While scientists can see bacteria under a regular microscope, they need a high-powered electron microscope to see viruses. Viruses have a protective protein shell called a capsid that surrounds one or two strands of genetic material. Some viruses also have an outer envelope composed of lipids (compounds such as fat that do not dissolve in water) and surface proteins that help the virus attach to a host cell. These proteins often look like a fringe of spikes or knobs around the virus. That's all. No ribosomes. No plasmids. No mitochondria.

On its own, a virus is a bundle of genes searching for a host cell. The sole mission of a virus is to get inside a cell and turn it into a factory to produce new viruses. Viruses replicate—reproduce—at warp speed because they're so much simpler than bacteria. It takes a virus only a few hours to attack and enter a living cell, gain control of its reproductive machinery, and churn out a new generation. Each daughter virus quickly infects other host cells, which could be in the lungs or the blood or the brain.

Such rapid replication means that viruses have a very high rate of mutation, a random and spontaneous change in a piece of genetic code. Viruses contain either RNA or DNA, unlike organisms such as bacteria and animals, which contain both. When a genetic mutation occurs in a bacterium of a DNA virus, the cell usually repairs itself before it replicates. This means that new cells don't carry the mutation. But RNA viruses are too small to hold a cell repair program. So mutations that don't kill the RNA virus will be passed on to the next generation.

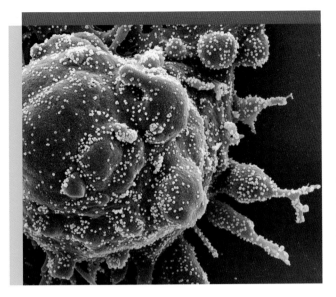

This electron micrograph shows a dying cell (green) infected with SARS-CoV-2 viruses (yellow).

RNA viruses are especially dangerous because of their constant and uncontrolled mutations. According to an article in the *New Yorker*, RNA viruses "are the fastest-evolving and most dangerous kinds of virus, and include the coronaviruses." Some genetic mutations help viruses adapt better to their environment or make them more dangerous to people. Influenza viruses—which are RNA viruses—mutate frequently. This means that scientists must develop a new vaccine to prevent flu each year.

PANDEMICS OF THE PAST AND PRESENT

Pandemics are not new. Ancient written records show that pandemics have occurred over many centuries. Historians believe that smallpox and bubonic plague likely triggered the earliest-recorded pandemics. Smallpox alone has caused an estimated one billion deaths since it first appeared around 300 BCE. However, most cases occurred centuries before medical science could positively identify smallpox. Pandemics have changed the course of history, especially three major historical pandemics: the bubonic plague, Spanish influenza, and AIDS, which is caused by the human immunodeficiency virus (HIV).

In the middle of the fourteenth century, the world population was about 450 million people. The bubonic plague, sometimes called the Black Death, wiped out between one-third and one-half of all Europeans between 1347 and 1351. The bacteria that cause bubonic plague live in fleas, which live on rats and other rodents. Italian traders returning from Asia brought the disease back with them, carried by flea-infected rats on their ships. Once docked, the rats jumped ship and entered cities and towns. Fleas on the infected rats moved to local rats that lived close to people. Fleas on those rats spread the plague to people. Once infected, people could transfer the plague to other people through close contact or could get it from the bites of infected fleas.

In the twenty-first century, plague still passes from fleas to rodents to people. Typically, fewer than ten Americans develop plague each year. Most are in New Mexico, Arizona, Colorado, and California, where wild rodents such as mice, chipmunks, and prairie dogs may carry plague-infected fleas. The fleas can jump onto hikers, campers, and other people living or working near the rodents. Most infected people recover from plague with antibiotics.

In the early twentieth century, another pandemic called Spanish flu ravaged Europe. The flu pandemic of 1918–1919 sickened up to one-third of the world's population and killed between fifty and one hundred million people. World War I (1914–1918) was nearly over, and many troops had been moving around the globe in crowded trains and ships. The flu virus—transmitted through droplets in the air when people sneeze, cough, or talk—traveled with them.

During the war, the governments of France, Britain, and the United States censored news reports about sick troops. They feared that such reports would alert the enemy to a weakened army and lead to military disaster. When flu reached Spain, a neutral country during World War I, newspapers reported widely on it, especially when Spain's King Alfonso XIII fell seriously ill. For the first time, the world heard about the pandemic, known from then on as the Spanish flu.

Scientists searched for the source of this pandemic for nearly a century. According to a 2014 *National Geographic* article, old Canadian medical records suggest the Spanish flu originated in China. In 1918 Britain formed the Chinese Labour Corps to bring in workers from China and send them to Europe to free up British soldiers for combat. Three thousand Chinese workers traveling by train across Canada became ill. Doctors in Canada, who held racist beliefs about the Chinese, said they were just lazy. These doctors gave the sick workers castor oil for their sore throats and sent them on their way.

Historians believe the workers likely carried the flu to Europe. The Chinese workers arrived in England in January 1918 and were sent to France, where hundreds of them died of flu, and soldiers returning home then spread it around the world. The pandemic ended in 1919 as those who were infected either developed immunity to the virus or died from it.

HIV, the virus that causes AIDS, was first identified in the early 1980s. Since then, HIV has killed about 32 million people. HIV

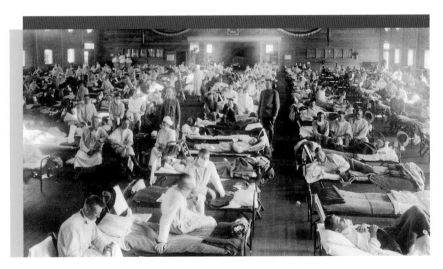

The Spanish flu (1918–1919) infected and killed millions. So many people were sick that spaces in hospitals and military bases quickly became crowded.

damages the body's immune system, so diseases and infections become more difficult to fight off. If HIV weakens the immune system enough, the body develops AIDS and needs extra help to fight off sicknesses. The WHO strives to monitor and protect the health of all people in the world. According to the organization, 38 million people worldwide had HIV/AIDS in 2019. About 690,000 people died of AIDS-related illnesses such as infections and cancer that year. The Centers for Disease Control and Prevention (CDC) reports that 1.2 million Americans live with HIV, and 1 out of 7 people with HIV don't know they have it. Even with improved treatments, this pandemic is still a serious global threat. According to the CDC, Black and Latino gay and bisexual men comprise the population most at risk for HIV in the US. Access to health care has long been limited for ethnic minorities, putting them at greater risk for many chronic conditions and infectious diseases such as HIV and SARS-CoV-2 as well.

Researchers know that HIV began long before the 1980s. As scientists began tracking HIV's origins, evidence mounted that the deadly virus had circulated in sub-Saharan Africa for decades. Scientists believe that HIV came from a virus that jumped from chimpanzees to humans early in the twentieth century, possibly in Cameroon. They think that when a human hunter killed a chimpanzee infected with simian immunodeficiency virus, the chimpanzee's blood likely splashed into an open wound on the hunter's body. Human and chimpanzee DNA are similar enough that the simian immunodeficiency virus could transfer to the hunter's body and adapt to become HIV.

Some modern researchers believe medical care delivered by European doctors contributed to the spread of HIV/AIDS in parts of Africa. In the early twentieth century, European countries had begun colonizing Africa. They launched health campaigns to treat diseases that the colonizers developed while living in Africa. At that time, all syringes were made of glass. They were expensive, scarce, and difficult to sterilize. Medical staff used the same syringes and needles repeatedly.

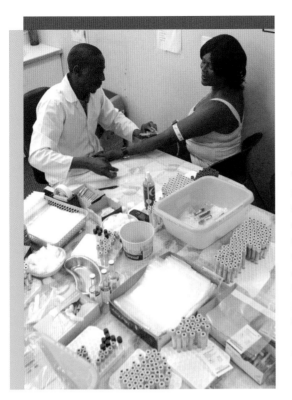

While HIV and AIDS continue to infect people around the world, doctors have developed several treatments to mitigate the symptoms of the virus. Because the virus harms patients' immune systems, it is crucial to protect patients from other diseases that their bodies would normally be able to fight off.

One doctor injected more than five thousand people in two years using the same six syringes without sterilizing them. It's almost certain that he infected many people with HIV with the contaminated syringes.

HIV/AIDS first appeared in the United States in the late 1970s although it was not immediately identified. The virus first struck gay men in Los Angeles, San Francisco, and New York City, leading some to call it a "gay" disease. Rampant homophobia dominated the government and much of the American population at the time and in the years that followed, slowing the identification and treatment of HIV/AIDS. Later research showed that straight people could also contract the virus. The virus had circulated in Africa, infecting people regardless of gender or sexual orientation, for many years. In the US, it posed a risk to all populations as well.

Since then, HIV/AIDS has continued to spread to every region of the world. Yet two-thirds of new cases of HIV infection in the

KNOW YOUR 'DEMICS

Epidemiologists—scientists who study infectious diseases—rate the severity of a particular disease occurring at a given time in one of four of these ways:

- *Outbreaks* strike a limited number of people in a limited area and last a short time. Monkeypox, a distant relative of smallpox, appeared for the first time in the United States in 2003. During the two-month outbreak, forty-seven people in six midwestern states caught monkeypox.
- *Endemics* are diseases that are always present in a region. For example, malaria is endemic in several countries in Africa such as Nigeria and Uganda.
- *Epidemics* hit a large number of people in several areas at the same time. In 2014–2015, scientists classified a major spread of Ebola virus disease as an epidemic because it infected large numbers of people in three countries in West Africa.
- *Pandemics* affect many people in many parts of the world at the same time. For example, the Spanish flu of 1918–1919, which sickened millions of people around the world, was a true pandemic.

twenty-first century occur in sub-Saharan Africa. Experts believe that multiple factors—such as poverty, war, inadequate medical care, mobile workforces, and polygyny (a social arrangement where a man marries more than one woman)—come together and make it difficult to control the spread of the disease.

During the early years of the pandemic, existing medications could not help patients with HIV. However, through the decades, scientists developed effective medications to treat the disease. The medications help protect the immune system so that people with

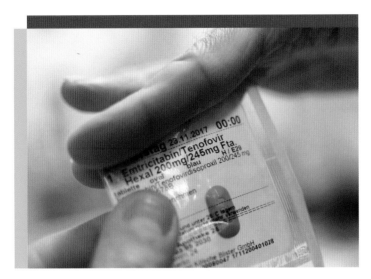

One lifesaving medication, known as PrEP, is taken before patients are exposed to HIV to prevent the virus from infecting them. People who are likely to be exposed should take PrEP every day.

HIV/AIDS can live a nearly normal life. In some cases, the medications are so effective that the virus cannot be detected in patients and may not even be transmitted. In 2012 the US Food and Drug Administration (FDA) approved a pill for pre-exposure prophylaxis (PrEP). When taken daily, the pill, which contains two medications, can keep people who do not have HIV but who are at high risk of getting it from becoming infected.

Until 2019 scientists were not sure what microbe would cause the next pandemic. Would it be a new bacterium that resists all available antibiotics? Would it be a new type of influenza, or even worse, a totally new virus to which people have no immunity? When COVID-19 appeared, answering these questions, it also confirmed what scientists knew already. Human activity is largely responsible for the spread of disease. Air travel, climate change, disruption of animal habitats, and human crowding have all contributed to the increase of zoonotic diseases—diseases that travel from animals to humans.

MEET THE CORONAVIRUSES

Coronaviruses are a large family of viruses named for projections from their surface that give the virus the appearance of a coronet, or crown. They're RNA viruses, so they're likely to mutate more often than a DNA virus. Coronaviruses circulate in people, birds, and animals including pigs, camels, and bats, sometimes causing serious diseases. A 1996 medical book said in its chapter about coronaviruses that "in humans, they [coronaviruses] are only proved to cause mild upper respiratory infections, i.e., common colds." Coronaviruses cause about one in five common colds as waves of infection pass through communities in the winter. The chapter goes on to say, "Immunity does not persist, and subjects may be re-infected, sometimes within a year." This twenty-five-year-old medical book foretold what concerned researchers are discovering in light of the COVID-19 pandemic: that it may be challenging to prevent reinfection even after a vaccine has been developed.

Scientists have had to rewrite the book on coronaviruses. Four of the seven coronaviruses known to infect people cause only mild to moderate disease—colds and pneumonia. However, three others can cause serious and even fatal diseases in people. As people increasingly came into contact with exotic animals (sometimes infected by bats) through illegal animal trade, wet markets, and disruption of animal habitats, these newly identified coronaviruses began to move from animals to people. SARS-CoV-1 appeared in 2002 and disappeared by 2004. MERS-CoV was identified in 2012. It continues to cause occasional localized outbreaks, especially in Saudi Arabia. In 2019 the third newly identified coronavirus, named SARS-CoV-2, emerged to cause the disease known as COVID-19, the first pandemic of the twenty-first century.

SEVERE ACUTE RESPIRATORY SYNDROME (SARS-COV-1)

Kwan Sui-chu, a seventy-eight-year-old Canadian grandmother, didn't know she was carrying the first new disease of the twenty-first century when she flew from Hong Kong back home to Canada in February 2003. Although she felt well, a dangerous virus lurked deep within her lungs. Kwan and her husband had spent two weeks visiting their sons in Hong Kong. They'd checked into Hong Kong's Metropole Hotel for a few nights on February 18 before their flight home. The reasonably priced hotel drew many international tourists.

Kwan returned to the apartment she shared with her family in Canada. At first, she felt well but soon developed a high fever, muscle aches, and a cough. Kwan's doctor prescribed rest and antibiotics. That didn't help. Kwan died at home a few days later of what her doctor said was a heart attack. But Kwan had really died of SARS, a disease spread by coughing, sneezing, and touching contaminated surfaces. She infected several family members before the new disease even had a name. The day after she died, one of her sons went to the emergency

In some countries, wearing masks in public was common practice to help prevent the spread of colds and flu even before the COVID-19 pandemic. In other countries where this practice was less common, the pandemic convinced many people to wear masks in public during future flu seasons, even after the COVID-19 pandemic ends.

room with breathing problems. The staff treated him with a nebulizer, a machine that turns liquid medication into a mist so the patient can breathe it in. The man inhaled the medicated mist and then exhaled millions of the new viruses each time he breathed out. His visit led to 128 cases of SARS among hospital personnel and their contacts.

However, SARS didn't start with Kwan. The first cases of the mysterious new illness broke out among people who had purchased wildlife from a wet market in Guangzhou, a city of more than thirteen million people in China's Guangdong Province. The close proximity of so many wild animals at the market allowed pathogens such as the SARS virus to pass from animal to animal and then to people.

Dozens of cases of the disease broke out in Guangzhou during November and December 2002 and into January 2003. The still-unnamed disease caused headaches, high fever, severe coughing, and bloody sputum. At its worst, the disease damaged lungs so badly they could no longer provide enough oxygen to the body. At first,

Chinese authorities didn't acknowledge the new disease. Instead, the Guangzhou media advised people to spray vinegar into the air in their houses to kill the virus. Citizens rushed to buy vinegar, flu medication, and antibiotics. These "treatments" didn't help.

By early February, SARS had sickened more than three hundred people and killed five in Guangzhou. China finally reported the new disease to the WHO on February 10, 2003. Later that month, Liu Jianlun, who had just treated SARS patients in Guangzhou, went to Hong Kong for a family wedding. He checked into Hong Kong's Metropole Hotel on the same day and on the same floor as the Kwans. The next day Liu became very ill and went to a Hong Kong hospital. He died two weeks later. Liu infected Kwan and dozens of other people at the hotel by coughing and sneezing in hotel hallways and elevators. Soon guests at the hotel and health-care workers at local hospitals who cared for them became ill.

Like Kwan, many infected people traveled from Hong Kong to other countries and gave SARS to people along the way.

In March 2003, Dr. Gro Harlem Brundtland, then director-general of WHO, said, "This syndrome, SARS, is now a worldwide health threat." Due to the volume of international air travel, cases soon spread to the United States, Vietnam, Taiwan, Singapore, and several countries in Europe, as well as to Canada and mainland China. By the end of 2003, SARS had sickened more than eight thousand people and killed about eight hundred.

As Sonia Shah, science journalist and author, said, "Within twenty-four hours, the SARS virus from Liu had spread to five

HONG KONG'S METROPOLE HOTEL BECAME KNOWN AS GROUND ZERO IN THE SARS-COV-1 OUTBREAK OF 2003. BECAUSE OF THE BAD PUBLICITY SURROUNDING THE METROPOLE, THE HOTEL CHANGED ITS NAME TO METROPARK HOTEL KOWLOON.

Many researchers believe the SARS-CoV-1 virus originated in horseshoe bats.

countries. Ultimately, SARS appeared in thirty-two countries. Thanks to the miracle of air travel, one infected man [Liu Jianlun] seeded a global outbreak."

Scientists later determined that SARS, since renamed SARS-CoV-1, started when horseshoe bats infected other animals a few months or years before the disease broke out in Guangzhou. The bats carried evidence of a new coronavirus. The ferret badgers and civets in the Guangzhou market seemed to be especially vulnerable to the virus. As the virus spread among them, it likely mutated and became easily transmissible to humans.

The CDC stopped tracking SARS-CoV-1 cases in July 2003. However, cases still occur sporadically. Seven cases occurred early in 2004 in Beijing. Testing found SARS-CoV-1 was very similar to the virus found in civets, a small striped and spotted animal distantly related to the mongoose. Health officials in Guangdong ordered nearly four thousand civets in captivity to be slaughtered to prevent a viral outbreak.

SARS-CoV-1 is highly contagious. During the 2003 epidemic, it killed nearly one out of every ten people it infected. Yet it didn't turn into a global pandemic. Why? First, scientists identified the virus quickly once it became public. Well-equipped, well-staffed hospitals treated most of the patients. China closed schools and put thousands of people in quarantine to stop its spread. Experts quickly traced the contacts of each sick person to discover who they might have infected and put those people in quarantine as well. Lastly, people only seem to become contagious once the symptoms of SARS-CoV-1 first begin. So those patients can be identified and isolated right around the same time they begin to release SARS-CoV-1 into the air with every cough. This is different from many other diseases. For example, people with flu are infectious *before* symptoms appear. They can spread the virus for a day or more before they realize they're sick.

MIDDLE EAST RESPIRATORY SYNDROME (MERS-COV)

"By all appearances, the camel had a cold," journalist Erika Fry wrote in an article for an online magazine. "One of nine camels kept in a barn outside Jeddah, Saudi Arabia, the animal was sick and expelling nasal drainage. The camel's owner did what he could to help, swabbing his own finger in vapor rub and applying it inside the dromedary's nose."

The sixty-year-old camel farmer developed a runny nose and cough. Five days later, he had trouble breathing. His local hospital transferred him to the Dr. Soliman Fakeeh Hospital, a large private medical center in Jeddah. Soon the man developed severe shortness of breath and doctors moved him into the hospital's intensive care unit. Then he got pneumonia and his kidneys failed. The man died in June 2012, eleven days after admission to the hospital.

The camel, however, recovered.

The man was the first known patient with MERS-CoV. Dr. Ali Mohamed Zaki, a virologist at the Fakeeh Hospital, collected blood and sputum samples from the man. As required by law, Zaki sent sputum samples to the Saudi Ministry of Health to check for the dangerous flu known as H1N1. The specimens were negative for H1N1. After the patient died, Zaki continued to search for the virus's identity. He soon discovered the virus was a coronavirus, but not SARS-CoV-1. "This was the first evidence that I could be dealing with a novel human coronavirus that had not been described before," Zaki told a journalist. He sent samples to another lab, which confirmed the new coronavirus. Nearly a year after being identified in 2012, the virus had a new name: Middle East respiratory syndrome. Like Li and his recognition of a new coronavirus in China in 2019, Zaki faced an attack by his government's health authorities. The Saudi government asked him to resign, and he did, right after he left the country.

Scientists linked the first patient and a few more that soon followed to close contact with camels. Researchers needed to know more. A 2014 study of camel blood and tissues showed the virus had been

The Saudi government advised people who worked with camels to wear masks around camels and to avoid touching them. In defiance of this, some owners kissed their camels.

THE CORONAVIRUSES AND INFLUENZA

NAME	YEAR IDENTIFIED	CASES IN WORLD	DEATHS	FATALITY RATE (%)	NUMBER OF COUNTRIES
SARS-CoV-1	2002	8,096	774	9.6	29
MERS-CoV	2012	2,442	858	35	27
SARS-CoV-2 (COVID-19)*	2019	124,955,308	2,746,397	2.2	Global
Influenza pandemic of 1918–1919	1918	Est. 500 million	Est. approx. 18 to 50 million	20	Global
Seasonal influenza†	Yearly	5 million severe cases, up to 1 billion total	290,000 to 646,000	0.1	Global

*as of March 2021
†estimated worldwide

Sources: Data from "SARS Basics Fact Sheet," CDC (2017); "Middle East Respiratory Syndrome Coronavirus (MERS-CoV)," WHO (accessed March 2021); Coronavirus Resource Center, Johns Hopkins (accessed March 2021); "Influenza: Are We Ready?" WHO (accessed March 2021); "Influenza (Seasonal)," WHO (November 6, 2018).

around in camels since at least 1992. Scientists believe that MERS-CoV spilled over from bats to camels somewhere in East Africa. Camels are common in many Middle Eastern and African countries and are used for transportation and for meat and milk. They may have gotten MERS-CoV from bat droppings or by eating figs and other fruit that infected bats had fed on.

MERS-CoV is not as contagious as SARS CoV-1. However, it kills about 35 percent of the people it infects, compared to a fatality rate of 9.6 percent for SARS CoV-1. MERS-CoV reached twenty-seven countries, although most of the cases occurred in Saudi Arabia. The virus causes fever, cough, and shortness of breath. Often kidney failure also occurs. However, some people have no symptoms or only mild cold-like symptoms. Patients with other medical conditions such as diabetes or heart disease are more likely to die from MERS-CoV than younger, healthier people. Scattered cases of MERS-CoV continue to occur in the Middle East.

Virologists—scientists who specialize in the study of viruses—say SARS-CoV-2 has several worrisome characteristics that set it apart from MERS-CoV and SARS-CoV-1. First, the virus spreads very easily. All it takes is breathing in respiratory droplets while talking with an infected person. Second, the virus spreads fast but not too fast. Viruses that immediately kill those they infect soon run out of people to infect and quickly die out. SARS-CoV-2 moves at just the right speed to allow it to continually infect new people without killing off too many of those it has infected. Next, SARS-CoV-2 can be passed before infected people show symptoms, or even in cases where infected people experience no symptoms at all. And when SARS-CoV-2 makes someone really sick, they may need weeks of intensive medical care, which threatens to overwhelm the health-care system. An NPR article says the world had never seen a pandemic caused by such a dangerous coronavirus. Virologists believe when these traits are combined into one virus, it makes for a perfect storm.

CHAPTER 4
GOING VIRAL

Bats carry more than sixty viruses that can infect people. These viruses can spill over into human populations when people disrupt bat habitats by cutting down forests, planting crops, and building houses. SARS-CoV-1 and MERS-CoV reached people when bats infected animals—probably civets in the case of SARS-CoV-1 and camels in MERS-CoV. Researchers believe horseshoe bats may have infected animals called pangolins living in the Wuhan area, leading to SARS-CoV-2 infection. Possibly the new coronavirus infection reached humans when they handled pangolins. However SARS-CoV-2 reached humans, it didn't take long for it to leave China and reach the rest of the world.

PATIENT ZERO

When a new disease breaks out, scientists always try to find patient zero, or the first person infected, to figure out where the disease

WE NEED BATS

Some people may wonder why we don't eliminate bats. They're responsible for carrying diseases that transfer to animals and then to people. These diseases include Ebola, SARS-CoV-1, MERS-CoV, and SARS-CoV-2. But bats do far more good than harm. Insect-eating bats can snap up twelve hundred mosquitoes an hour and can eat their body weight in bugs each night. Bats that eat fruit and nectar help to pollinate flowers, just as bees do. Bats pollinate over five hundred different plants. The world is better off with bats than without them.

came from. In the case of SARS-CoV-2, Chinese scientists believe patient zero may have been a fifty-five-year-old man in China who became ill on November 17, 2019. While SARS-CoV-2 had not been identified at the time, later blood tests showed the man had been infected with the new virus. By the end of December 2019, the virus had infected more than 180 people in China. On January 13, 2020, officials confirmed a case of SARS-CoV-2 in Thailand in a woman who had traveled to China. It's believed to be the first recorded case outside of China. And on January 20, a Washington State man became the first known person in the United States to develop COVID-19 when he returned home from China after visiting relatives in Wuhan.

Possibly the virus had been sickening people in China before November 17, before January 13 in Thailand, and before January 20 in the US. Doctors might have thought their patients had pneumonia. At first, doctors had no reason to suspect a new disease or to report anything unusual. But soon the world realized that something was terribly wrong.

COVID-19 IN THE UNITED STATES

The first known case of COVID-19 in the US was identified January 2020 in the state of Washington. The patient was a man who had recently traveled to Wuhan, China. By March 1, the virus had reached New York City. Researchers said that the virus began spreading in New York weeks before March 1 and that the virus came from Europe. Between February 1 and March 17, an estimated one million passengers on ten thousand flights arrived in American airports from heavily infected European countries.

However, the US government blamed China for the new virus and banned flights from China but not those from Europe. That decision was largely based on racist beliefs. Trump continually accused China of bringing the virus to the US. But research showed that the failure to ban European flights to the US most likely contributed to the rapid spread of the virus in this country.

Adriana Heguy, director of the Genome Technology Center at NYU Langone Health, said, "We know with certainty that these [American cases] were coming from European strains. That our first case was community acquired gave us the hint that [COVID-19] has been going around for a while and it was just undetected because there was no testing happening before."

COVID-19 hit Europe hard. By late March, COVID-19 was killing more than nine hundred people each day in Italy alone. European leaders developed strong national responses to the pandemic. Entire countries shut down travel, residents were restricted to their homes, and businesses closed. For example, the pandemic hit Italy especially hard in the spring of 2020. By July, Italian cases of COVID-19 were among the lowest in Europe. According to a *New York Times* article, science guided the Italian government. Prime Minister Giuseppe Conte put the country into a total lockdown for several months. "The health of the Italian people comes and will always come first," he said when he extended the shutdown into October.

THE PANDEMIC TIMELINE OF 2020

The *American Journal of Managed Care* published a timeline that covered the first twelve months of the pandemic. These are some of the major events:

JANUARY 9 The WHO announced the presence of unusual coronavirus pneumonia in Wuhan.

JANUARY 21 The CDC confirmed the first US case.

JANUARY 31 The WHO issued a global health emergency.

FEBRUARY 2 Global air travel was restricted.

FEBRUARY 3 The US declared a public health emergency.

FEBRUARY 10 The Chinese death toll exceeded that of SARS-CoV-1.

MARCH 1 The WHO declared COVID-19 a pandemic.

MAY 28 The US death toll passed one hundred thousand.

JUNE 30 US cases predicted to hit one hundred thousand per day.

JULY 7 The US reported three million total infections.

JULY 27 Congress introduced a stimulus package that would provide economic relief to US citizens.

AUGUST 17 COVID-19 became the third-leading cause of death in the US, with deaths exceeding one thousand per day.

SEPTEMBER 23 A more contagious strain of COVID-19 was discovered.

OCTOBER 19 The world reached forty million cases of COVID-19 and 1.1 million deaths.

NOVEMBER 16 Pharmaceutical company Moderna revealed its vaccine had a 94.5 percent efficacy rate. Two days later, Pfizer and BioNTech revealed their vaccine had a 95 percent efficacy rate.

DECEMBER 10 The FDA endorsed the Pfizer and BioNTech vaccine.

DECEMBER 17 The FDA endorsed the Moderna vaccine.

DECEMBER 31 The CDC reported that 2.8 million Americans had received the first portion of a COVID-19 vaccine.

In Denmark, new strains of the coronavirus were detected in minks on fur farms. The government ordered that all the minks, numbering in the millions, be killed to protect humans from the new virus strains.

However, in the United States, Trump left the pandemic response up to the governors of individual states. And some governors left the response up to mayors and local health departments. American actions were haphazard, chaotic, and all too often based on political leanings rather than science. According to the Pew Research Center, far more Democrats than Republicans have confidence in scientists. And the majority of Democrats want scientific experts involved in developing health-care policy, while more than half of Republicans believe scientists should stay out of policy debates.

People with more conservative beliefs seemed less likely to believe in or comply with recommendations from health officials. Some thought that SARS-CoV-2 was not very serious or that it was some kind of conspiracy theory. People with liberal beliefs were more likely to believe in the science of infectious disease. But the SARS-CoV-2 virus really didn't care much about politics. By March 26, one thousand Americans had died of the disease. If the US government had consisted of strong leadership that believed in science rather than rumors and chaos, could the course of the pandemic have been shortened or at least moderated in some way?

LOCKED DOWN, LOCKED OUT

A few state governments did begin to take some of the steps that had helped Europe gain control over the virus. For example, the California governor issued the nation's first stay-at-home order in early March. It required California's nearly forty million residents to remain in their homes except to seek medical care, obtain food, or to help sick or elderly relatives. Essential workers were allowed to leave home. These included people working in health care, grocery stores, pharmacies, and other vital jobs. California citizens largely complied with this first lockdown. More states soon followed California's example. In the weeks that followed, millions of people began to work from home, linking to their workplaces by computer and video.

Stay-at-home orders were especially effective in New York City, one of the first hot spots of the pandemic in the US. The city shut down for about twelve weeks. Experts say that action reduced COVID-19 cases in the city by 70 percent. Initially, it seemed the country could control the spread of COVID-19. Cases were stable through April, May, and June.

While the stay-at-home order did slow the spread of COVID-19, the US and the global economy plummeted. Millions of people in the US alone lost their jobs because they couldn't work from home, the places where they had worked closed down, or their employer couldn't afford to keep them on the payroll. The US economy lost billions of dollars in sales of products and services, and in wages and taxes not paid.

Joblessness and unemployment claims rose to the highest levels ever. Many states extended their unemployment insurance programs, providing additional funds for longer periods than usual. Congress passed a stimulus package to assist individuals, businesses, and local governments with their financial needs. It provided the following:

- $1,200 checks to individuals, based on their income
- $130 billion for hospitals for ventilators and other equipment
- Extended unemployment insurance for millions of workers
- $150 billion for state and local government
- An expansion of lending for corporations
- Interest-free loans for small businesses

These funds helped some people and some businesses for a while, but others received little or no help. As the weeks went on, many people could not keep up with their rent or mortgage payments. The majority of states put a temporary ban on evictions, which might have saved up to forty million people from being evicted. However, experts estimated that after the bans expired, more than 430,000 cases of COVID-19 and nearly eleven thousand deaths resulted. Some people became homeless, while others moved in with family and friends. Both actions increased the risk of getting COVID-19. Evictions and job losses led to widespread hunger. An estimated fifty million Americans faced hunger. One in four of them were children. People often had to rely on food banks and organizations that distributed free food to feed their families.

By the middle of June, people were tired of the restrictions on their activities and livelihoods. Businesses insisted on the right to reopen their doors. Customers wanted to shop in their favorite stores and to eat out whenever and wherever they wanted to. People who could not work at home demanded the right to return to work. And those without jobs needed to look for work.

Because the US didn't have a coherent national policy to handle the pandemic, these pressures fell on states and local leaders. Elected

After George Floyd was murdered by police in Minneapolis in May 2020, millions of protesters took to the streets all across the US and in other countries. Some expected a surge in COVID-19 cases as a result of these mass gatherings, but protesters practiced mask wearing, hand sanitizing, and social distancing. No spike in COVID-19 cases resulted as a consequence of these protests.

officials, concerned for their citizens and economies (and perhaps for the loss of their positions with the next election), gave in to the demands to lift lockdowns and reopen businesses. An Associated Press article said, "In a dispute that has turned nakedly political, President Donald Trump has been agitating to restart the economy, singling out Democratic-led states and egging on protesters who feel governors are moving too slowly." Politics, not science, guided far too many

"THE CORONAVIRUS PANDEMIC PITS ALL OF HUMANITY AGAINST THE VIRUS. THE DAMAGE TO HEALTH, WEALTH, AND WELL-BEING HAS ALREADY BEEN ENORMOUS. THIS IS LIKE A WORLD WAR, EXCEPT IN THIS CASE, WE'RE ALL ON THE SAME SIDE."

—Bill Gates, cofounder of Microsoft, 2020

decisions during the pandemic in the US. It was too soon to reopen stores, restaurants, gyms, and hair salons. It was too soon to return to business as normal. A second wave of COVID-19 cases surged.

Over the summer, as states and cities eased restrictions, people thought it was safe to go out more often. Then scientists learned about super-spreading events, where large numbers of people gathered and outbreaks of COVID-19 occurred among them. These events played a big role in the spread of COVID-19. For example, sixteen friends who met for a June birthday party at a Florida bar all came down with COVID-19, as did seven employees. Partygoer Erika Crisp posted on Facebook, "Welp, Florida opened back up and my butt should've stayed home this past weekend cause I just tested positive for the damn COVID. #IKnowBetter #MyFault #WearYourMasksPeople."

In mid-July, the US passed the grim milestone of four million cases of COVID-19. It took one hundred days for cases to reach one million, forty-five days to reach two million, twenty-seven days to reach three million, and fifteen days to reach four million. Restaurants and shops and other businesses opened, then closed, then opened again, sometimes within days, as COVID-19 cases surged upward and then decreased. COVID-19 continued to spread around the world as well. During a media briefing on July 27, 2020, Tedros Adhanom Ghebreyesus, director-general of the WHO, said, "This is the sixth time a global health emergency has been declared under the International Health Regulations, but it is easily the most severe. And the pandemic continues to accelerate."

"THE PATIENTS KEEP COMING. BEDS FILL UP. VENTILATORS GET PARCELED OUT. QUICKLY, THERE ARE MANY MORE PATIENTS THAN EQUIPMENT AND SPACE. WHO GETS THE PRECIOUS FEW VENTILATORS?"
—Dr. Helen Ouyang, Columbia University, 2020

COVID-19 HITS MINORITY GROUPS HARD

Across the United States, Black and Latinx Americans were three times more likely to become infected with coronavirus than white people. Other reports said that Black Americans, Indigenous people, Pacific Islanders, and Latinx Americans were also three times more likely to die from COVID-19 than white Americans were, and that Black and Latinx Americans were hospitalized nearly five times more often as white Americans.

One facet of racial inequality is how health-care professionals and institutions historically discriminated against and continue to underserve people of color. Generations of this inequality have led to higher rates of chronic illnesses among Black Americans and Indigenous people. Factors that add to the disparity include lack of health insurance and crowded housing. Also—particular to this pandemic—people of color make up a larger portion of essential workers, such as those in housekeeping, agriculture, and food service, who cannot work at home during the pandemic.

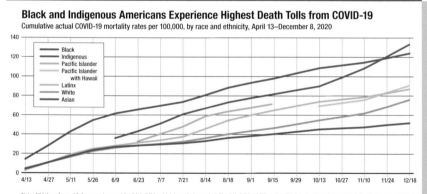

Black and Indigenous Americans Experience Highest Death Tolls from COVID-19
Cumulative actual COVID-19 mortality rates per 100,000, by race and ethnicity, April 13–December 8, 2020

Note: All intervals are 14 days apart, except for 5/11–5/26, which is a 15-day period. The 9/1, 9/29, 10/27, and 11/24 data has been interpolated. Pacific Islander data prior to 10/13 did not include Hawaii, as it was not releasing data; its inclusion resulted in an overall drop in the Pacific Islander rate, which begins a new series at 10/13.
Source: APM Research Lab

Data that track deaths from COVID-19 by race show disparities between racial groups. These numbers do not take into account people who died from complications caused by the pandemic, but not necessarily from COVID-19 itself. With those figures, the disparities only grow.

WHAT SPREADS FASTER THAN COVID-19? RACIST ATTACKS

Asian Americans faced a torrent of hate and blame for COVID-19 in 2020, including from Trump, who persisted in calling SARS-CoV-2 the Chinese virus, the Wuhan virus, and the kung flu. Such verbiage encouraged others to be racist against Asian people. Those prejudiced against Chinese people usually didn't distinguish between different Asian cultures and extended their bigotry to Japanese and Korean people as well.

Chinese American Justin Tsui was a registered nurse studying for his doctorate in nursing at New York's Columbia University. Tsui was waiting to transfer subway trains when a man accosted him and blamed him and China for COVID-19, as another example of "all these sicknesses" supposedly spread by Chinese people. The man kept moving closer to Tsui, who was forced to step toward the edge of the platform. "I didn't think that if he shoved me into the tracks I'd have the physical energy to crawl back up," Tsui said. The man backed off when a bystander threatened to record the incident and call the police.

Abraham Choi, a Korean American, had a similar experience in New York's Penn Station. A man behind him coughed and spit on him. "You Chinese f—k," the man said. "All of you should die, and all of you have the Chinese virus." Choi waited for the man to leave and then reported the situation to a police officer. "I was told that spitting wasn't a crime, and that it wouldn't be worth the paperwork I would have to go through to take any sort of action," he said.

In July 2020, the CDC recognized and summarized the factors contributing to the increased risk of getting COVID-19 among minorities. They include:

- long-term discrimination in areas such as criminal justice, finance, housing, and education leading to chronic stress
- decreased access to health care due to lack of insurance through employment, and problems with transportation, child care, and cultural differences in accessing care
- more minorities employed in essential work settings that led to increased exposure to coronavirus
- gaps in education and income that may limit job opportunities and result in lower-paying jobs
- more likely to live in crowded, multigenerational households, which can lead to cross infection; a higher risk of eviction among this group during the pandemic
- higher rates of underlying medical conditions such as diabetes, high blood pressure, and obesity that increase the risk of severe illness if infected with coronavirus

The CDC offered guidance on what we can do to mitigate these inequities. "To prevent the spread of COVID-19, we must work together to ensure that people have resources to maintain and manage their physical and mental health, including easy access to information, affordable testing, and medical and mental health care. We need programs and practices that fit the communities where racial and minority groups live, learn, work, play, and worship."

CAPTIVE CRUISE SHIPS

On February 21, 2020, Terry Schultze and three friends living in Northern California boarded the luxury cruise ship, *Grand Princess*. The ship left San Francisco for a fifteen-day cruise to Hawaii with a

INTERNATIONAL HUMANITARIAN ORGANIZATION HELPS NAVAJO NATION

Doctors Without Borders (Médecins Sans Frontières, or MSF, in French), is an international medical humanitarian organization based in France. MSF arrived in New Mexico in May 2020 to help the 170,000-person Navajo Nation battle the coronavirus. Normally, MSF helps poorer countries around the world to fight diseases such as Ebola and malaria. This was MSF's first visit to the United States.

By that May, the Navajo Nation had one of the highest coronavirus death rates in the United States. "I'm scared for our languages, our culture, our people," Navajo physician Michelle Tom said. "And I know it's happening all around the world. I get that. . . . My time is limited on this Earth. But our language and our cultures can continue to live forever, as long as there are Navajo people. I think that's what scares me most."

MSF wrote in a news release that the US government had not given Indigenous communities enough resources to meet their health-care needs. Amy Segal, project coordinator, said, "While this resource gap has been well documented, there is no defensible reason for it to persist. The US has the ability and resources to improve the health system serving tribal nations. This is a solvable problem." A team of physicians, nurses, and health educators spent two months assisting the Navajo Nation and then left in late July 2020. Segal said, "We have provided some support to these efforts, but until the federal government does more to address core public health inequities, these communities will remain extremely at-risk to devastation from this virus."

brief stop in Mexico before heading back to San Francisco. At least, that was the plan. On Wednesday, March 4, passengers woke up to find letters under their doors. "The letters said we would not be going to Mexico, but instead were heading home to San Francisco," Schultze said. The CDC was investigating a few cases of COVID-19 in Northern California among passengers of the previous trip on the *Grand Princess*.

The next day during lunch, "The captain came over the PA system to give us the latest reports and asked us to please return to our cabins when we finished lunch and remain there until further notice," Schultze said. Many passengers aboard the *Diamond Princess*, sister ship to the *Grand Princess*, had developed COVID-19 after docking in Tokyo. "We had heard of the virus," Schultze said. "The *Diamond Princess* was all over the news. We knew how bad it was, but it was on the other side of the world, so we went ahead with our cruise."

The ship made it back to San Francisco but couldn't dock. "We stayed about ten miles [1.6 km] off the coast. Government authorities said they would prefer we stayed out there. I kept using the term 'circling the drain' because we had no idea what would happen to us," Schultze said. Meanwhile, the California National Guard brought coronavirus test kits to the ship by helicopter. Nineteen crew members and two passengers tested positive for the coronavirus. Health officials wouldn't allow the *Grand Princess* to dock in San Francisco but sent the ship to a commercial dock in Oakland. More than three thousand passengers and crew members would be quarantined—the passengers on land and the crew at sea.

"They bused some of us to Travis Air Force Base in Fairfield, California and others to a base in Southern California," Schultze said. The passengers remained in quarantine at Travis for fourteen days. "People came to our room to take our temperature twice a day. Our meals were good and we could go outside for fresh air and to walk. There was a chain link fence around the hotel with guards on the other side.

"All in all, it was not a bad experience. The *Grand Princess* staff, the Travis staff, and the CDC treated us with respect and dignity. They took very good care of us." Even so, Schultze was delighted to get home to her husband, Don, and their dog, Dixie. "We were gone thirty-two days total: eighteen on the ship and fourteen at Travis."

By May 2020 more than forty cruise ships from several countries had cases of coronavirus. Thousands of passengers experienced delays in landing or were quarantined. Thousands more crew members remained on board the ships. Often their home countries refused to accept them, borders were closed, or plane flights were canceled. CDC regulations would not allow crew members to disembark and stay at public hotels. It was too expensive to the cruise lines to take the crew members home. The virus held thousands of people hostage at sea.

CHAPTER 5
SCHOOL'S OUT!

The lockdowns that swept across the country affected everyone, including kids, teens, and young people. Most lost the last few months of school during the spring of 2020. And as summer turned into fall, most schools elected to continue online learning or distance learning for at least part of the 2020–2021 year. Many teachers, school officials, and parents feared there was no safe way to return to school during the pandemic. While experts didn't always agree on the effectiveness of distance learning versus in-person learning at school, teens had a lot to say about it.

KIDS AT HOME

"The hardest thing about being home all the time is that I easily become bored," fourteen-year-old Charlotte Bentley said in May 2020. "I used to

stay entertained and busy with school, but now I'm doing online school, and I work at my own pace. Once I finish, I go on my phone for a while, but even that gets pretty boring." She especially worries about math. "It's much harder learning math through a YouTube video than in person. I already struggle with math, so I assume it will be harder to learn 9th grade math when I start school again." Charlotte didn't know at the time that she'd be starting high school online as well.

Charlotte missed her friends but was glad she has sisters. "When the government issues the all clear and we can go out again, the first thing I'll do is go shopping for new clothes or go out to eat with my best friend. I feel bad for all the kids and teens out there with no siblings to talk to while quarantined. I have two sisters, and they make quarantine much more fun! We go swimming, make TikToks, and hang out every day."

Fourteen-year-old Aidan Kirkman finished ninth grade with distance learning. He found both positives and negatives in the experience.

The hardest part of staying home through this pandemic is being stuck with the same people. We are all beginning to get on each other's nerves and we argue almost every day. It could just be as simple as having a snack. My sister and I both go for the same thing and then next thing we know we're fighting over it.

The best part of being home all the time is, surprisingly, being with my family. Even though we argue a lot, when we're not arguing we have a lot of time to bond and become closer to each other. On the weekends we go for hikes in the mountains, and on the weekdays we often walk or bike around the park near our house for exercise.

The day that school closed I was at a track meet. It was my first varsity racing meet as a freshman. It really stung

Empty streets were a common sight early in the pandemic.

to know that the rest of my season would be gone. What I miss most about school are all the things I could have experienced during the last few months: from having a full season of track to just being with friends at lunch enjoying our break. I decided to keep a journal so I could remember what the pandemic was like. I don't normally keep a journal, but I feel I'm living through something historical and I want to be able to remember what it was like later in life.

When this is over I plan to do something with my friends. I really just want to do something fun with the people I choose to be near, not who I'm forced to be near. My friends are a large part of my life and it feels like that part was taken from me very suddenly. Having school online has allowed me to move at my own pace without distractions. This makes it easier for me to do all my work in less time, allowing me to have more free time in the afternoon when I finish.

Distance learning affected teachers as well as students. Fourth-grade teacher Amy Jacobsen said of the 2019–2020 school year, "This is not normal teaching. . . . We know the curriculum. We've done our research. It's just the platform and how to present the information and ensure that the students understand it." She missed the relationships with her students. "You can read a kid in class. You can't do that through a screen. Distance learning is not ideal. It's not sustainable."

COLLEGE AT HOME

Students entering college for the first time were at a particular disadvantage. Missing the milestones of senior year in high school was bad enough. But not being able to plan for college was a real hardship. Leaving home and family and preparing to move into a college dorm to start a new life is a big part of growing up for many older teens.

Mia Harton was seventeen in the spring of 2020 when she had to leave school before her senior year was up. "I missed several senior school events such as the senior barbeque, banquet, and other activities," she said. "I missed our spring sports." She also lost the summer job she'd counted on to help out with college expenses. Even so, Mia knew she was lucky. "None of my family or friends were infected by the coronavirus. I'm happy that I got to spend this time with my family before I headed off to college. This experience brought us closer together and now I know not to take anything for granted."

But the pandemic wasn't done with Mia. She'd planned to enter Temple University in Philadelphia, Pennsylvania, in the fall of 2020. "I was unable to attend accepted students day at Temple and had to do my freshman orientation online as well," she said." Mia moved into her dorm in August, but after one week, Temple said all classes would be online. A few days later, the university told students to return home for online classes. "We'd been watching as cases at other universities increased, doubling almost every day," Mia said. "Based

Throughout the country, students had to begin taking classes at home using video conference software.

on how surrounding schools reacted to the rise in positive cases it wasn't a surprise that we would be online so soon in the school year."

Distance learning affected teachers at every level. JaNay Brown-Wood is an author and assistant professor of child and adolescent development at California State University, Sacramento. "Flexible online classes allow students to check in and complete their work as they see fit, as long as they keep to the deadlines," she said. "Disadvantages include the increased amount of screen time and the fatigue that comes with being plugged into a device for long periods. I worry about the effect this might have on students' vision, posture, physical activity levels, and mental health. In addition, distance learning often lacks the dynamic interactions and conversations that happen in a classroom. Preparing quality distance learning experiences takes an immense amount of time, especially if you want to provide meaningful engagement for your students." Brown-Wood missed the immediate, face-to-face student feedback she got from in-person learning. "I've always thrived on interacting directly with my students and a lot of that is lost with distance learning. It's difficult to build the same types of relationships with distance learning."

Millions of students and teachers echo these stories. One virus changed so many lives, and not for the better. Would very young children learn the social skills they need to get along in the world if much of their early education took place at home rather than with their peer groups? Nearly three-fourths of lower-income families and over half of higher-income families worried their children would fall behind academically.

Will there be a large number of "COVID kids" who have gaps in their emotional development and in their education as well? According to NPR, as many as three million students may have dropped out of school, most of them because they lack internet access. Alex, a teacher in Virginia who asked that NPR not share her last name, said of these trends, "It is really, really unsettling. I think people don't realize how much we need to see these kids. A lot of times in schools, we are the first line for seeing signs of child abuse, for seeing signs of food insecurity. And you don't have that with virtual students."

BY SPRING OF 2021, MOST STATES LIFTED ORDERS FOR SCHOOLS TO REMAIN CLOSED, AND MANY SCHOOLS OFFERED BOTH IN-PERSON AND ONLINE INSTRUCTION.

Distance learning also heavily affected parents. In November 2020, *Forbes* wrote, "School shutdowns are occurring all over the country. Working parents bear the brunt of this order. Their lives are turned upside down. Some parents face a hard choice—keeping a job or taking care of their children. It was reported by the National Women's Law Center that between August and September, over 800,000 women left the workforce to look after their children." Parents who were able to work at home had to juggle their jobs by virtual connections.

Meanwhile, they had to watch their children and supervise their virtual education. It was a no-win situation for so many families.

As fall approached, some schools planned to move from distance learning to in-person classes. But cases among children and young people started to rise in the late summer and early fall of 2020 as students of all ages returned to classes. Some schools and colleges were only open for days before COVID-19 infections increased. As cases mounted, many schools and colleges closed again. Classrooms were once again empty, and college dorms cleared out as millions of students returned home again for distance learning.

However, months of distance learning led to serious problems for many families. Lisa (last name not given) said that distance learning and isolation changed her extroverted thirteen-year-old son in ways she never expected. His grades slipped and he began to withdraw. "Next

COVID-19 tests were usually in high demand, but before the winter holidays of Thanksgiving and Christmas, many waited for hours in their cars to receive a test, hoping to feel safe enough to travel and visit family.

he was telling us he couldn't make himself do the work, that he didn't want to disappoint us all the time, that he was worthless," she said.

During periods of intense stress, such as a pandemic, young people may become very anxious and worried about themselves, their friends, and their parents. They may ask: Will I get sick? How about my parents? When can I see my friends again? Will I still have friends when this is all over? Instead of planning for the future, young people have had to put their lives on indefinite hold. And the enforced social isolation and loneliness during the pandemic may affect young people for years to come.

The CDC reported that emergency room visits for mental health issues such as stress, anxiety, and even self-injury increased by nearly one-fourth in children aged 5–11, and nearly one-third among those aged 12–17. One survey showed that 30 percent of high school students

By 2021, as teachers began getting vaccinated, public schools reopened across the country according to state guidelines. Teachers and students wore masks and practiced social distancing as best as possible. Bumping elbows became a common replacement for high fives and handshakes.

felt unhappy and depressed during the pandemic. And a quarter of young people aged 18 to 24 said they had seriously considered suicide during the pandemic.

Therapist Sharon Young explains it this way. "Everything that used to be familiar and give structure to their lives, and predictability, and normalcy, is gone," she said. "Kids need all these things even more than adults do, and it's hard for them to feel emotionally safe when they're no longer there."

Stanford Children's Hospital recommends friends and parents watch for these symptoms in children and teens. They may signal the need for mental health intervention. The child or teen is

- being more irritable or easily annoyed than usual
- lashing out
- avoiding their friends
- sleeping too much or not sleeping enough
- overeating or not eating enough
- not enjoying things they usually like

Teachers were also at risk of catching COVID-19 in the classroom. In September 2020 thirty-four-year-old teacher AshLee DeMarinis of Missouri died of COVID-19. Her sister, Jennifer Heissenbuttel, said DeMarinis was nervous about going back to school. "She was a great teacher," Heissenbuttel said of her sister. "She taught special education. She taught the kids life skills, things that they would learn, need to do everyday activities down to, like, learning how to write out a check." Heissenbuttel spoke of her last minutes with her sister. "I just sat with her. I told her that our family loved her, that I would make sure that everything was taken care of."

As the months went on, schools opened and closed, often several times. People in the US and around the world wondered if and when in-person school would be safe for students and their teachers.

CHAPTER 6

FLATTENING THE CURVE

FOR YOUR COUNTRY RIGHT NOW AND FOR THE WAR THAT WE'RE IN AGAINST [COVID-19], I'M ASKING YOU TO DO FOUR SIMPLE THINGS: WEAR A MASK, SOCIAL DISTANCE, WASH YOUR HANDS, AND BE SMART ABOUT CROWDS. I'M NOT ASKING SOME OF AMERICA TO DO IT. WE ALL GOTTA DO IT.

—Dr. Robert Redfield, then director of the CDC, 2020

The COVID-19 pandemic brought with it several phrases new to many of us, such as "flattening the curve." Epidemiologists use that term to compare how an infection might spread if society took no steps to slow the spread to what might happen if society does slow the spread. A graph showing the spread of a disease such as COVID-19 starts with a horizontal line in the middle representing hospital capacity. The faster the curve, or peak of infection, rises, the more likely that hospitals will run out of supplies, that doctors and nurses won't be able to keep up with patient volume, and that patients may not get into a hospital at all or may not get a bed in an intensive care unit if they need one.

"If you look at the curves of outbreaks . . . they go up big peaks, and then they come down. What we need to do is flatten that down," Dr. Anthony Fauci, director of the National Institute of Allergy and

Infectious Diseases, said. "That would have less people infected [and fewer] deaths. You do that by trying to interfere with the natural flow of the outbreak."

Health-care experts say flattening the curve is not difficult. A robust government plan for addressing the pandemic, plus a population armed with the knowledge, tools, and support they need to help, is the best combination to slow the spread. But with no cure for COVID-19, no vaccine to prevent it (at the time), and a government unwilling to provide support to its citizens during a crisis, health professionals in 2020 had to rely on individuals to follow basic guidelines in an effort to slow the spread. These were simple activities that everyone could do: wearing face masks when outside the home, maintaining social distancing of at least 6 feet (2 m) when waiting in a crowd, and washing hands frequently.

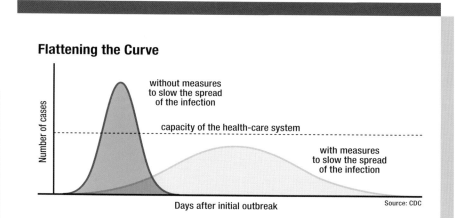

Flattening the Curve

without measures to slow the spread of the infection

capacity of the health-care system

with measures to slow the spread of the infection

Number of cases

Days after initial outbreak

Source: CDC

Let's say a million people get COVID-19 within four weeks. The graphic's tall pointed curve shows that when many people get sick during a short period of time, they quickly overwhelm the health-care system. Then let's say the flatter curve also represents one million people who get COVID-19, but spread over ten weeks because society worked to slow the disease's spread. While the same number of people get COVID-19, they get it over a longer period of time, and the number of patients at a given time do not overwhelm the health-care system.

Anthony Fauci, director of the National Institute of Allergy and Infectious Diseases, speaks at a task force conference in March 2020, shortly after the pandemic takes hold in the United States.

MASKS WORK

"We're seeing a rollercoaster in the United States," said Dr. Christopher Murray, director of the University of Washington's Institute for Health Metrics and Evaluation. "It appears that people are wearing masks and socially distancing more frequently as infections increase, then after a while as infections drop, people let their guard down and stop taking these measures to protect themselves and others—which, of course, leads to more infections." Scientists estimated that if 95 percent of people in the US wore masks every time they left home, coronavirus deaths could drop 49 percent.

By July 2020, many governors and mayors mandated that everyone must wear face masks outside their homes. Some of the nation's biggest retailers required customers to wear masks to shop in their stores. Most

WHO WEARS MASKS?

National Geographic published the results of a poll about who did and who did not wear masks. The poll found people who reported wearing masks

- were more often female than male
- were ages 18–34, and 65 and over
- were more liberal
- had higher levels of education and higher incomes
- were more often people of color than white people

people felt the minor discomfort of wearing face masks was a small price to pay to help prevent the spread of COVID-19 among their families, friends, and communities. Wearing face masks can reduce the risk of exposure to COVID-19 by 70 percent or more, according to the CDC. Masks block some of the particles that a person breathes into or from the open air, offering protection to the mask wearer and to other people as well. Good-quality surgical masks (available online) and two-layered fabric masks are both effective. Masks must cover the nose and the mouth to work. Some experts recommend wearing at least two masks to reduce the chance of transmission even further. Face shields, sheets of clear plastic that users wear over their whole face, are not a good substitute for masks.

Some people felt wearing face masks impinged on their personal rights, saying it wasn't up to them to prevent the spread of the disease. (Then who is it up to, if not all of us?) Even when states required a mask, some people refused. When a Costco employee told a man without a mask to leave, he said, "I got every f—ing right to not wear a mask. This isn't about wearing a mask, it's about control." News reports were filled with angry people screaming at store and restaurant

Protesters against mandatory vaccinations and government-imposed mask and social distancing rules took to the streets in Boston in August 2020. Such protests occurred in several state capitals throughout the summer. Most protesters at these events did not wear masks or practice social distancing.

employees who asked them to put on a mask or leave. Some of these anti-maskers didn't believe that masks worked or that the coronavirus even existed.

Science has proven the effectiveness of wearing masks to help prevent the spread of COVID-19. Even so, millions of people congregated in large groups on the beach, in the street, at parties, and in bars, refusing to wear masks. All too often, this resulted in outbreaks of COVID-19. Dr. Henry Redel, chief of infectious disease at Saint Peter's University Hospital in New Brunswick, New Jersey, said, "By wearing a mask you can protect the people around you, family, friends, and the general public. Not everyone is healthy, and many people have medical conditions and impaired immune systems. If we all want to get back to 'normal,' then wearing a mask is the way to do it, and it shows consideration for our communities."

Many of us have older parents and elderly grandparents we'd like to protect. We have friends with underlying medical conditions, such as Kris Obligar. Obligar is a twenty-seven-year-old speech therapy assistant in Sacramento, California. In July 2020, she and her parents came down with COVID-19. While her parents stayed home with mild cases, Obligar became very ill and entered an ICU. She has diabetes, which makes her more susceptible to infectious diseases. Obligar wants other people to learn from her experience.

I'll stick to a simple message for those that are still skeptical about COVID-19 and what could happen to you or someone you love: If you're ready to walk into an ER by yourself, be intubated by yourself, be extubated by yourself, wake up from severe sedatives without a familiar face around, then go on to recover in the hospital without a single hand to hold . . . then by all means please continue to not wear a mask, to go out, and not socially distance yourselves. Thankfully, I had a nursing staff that truly made me feel like family and even a doctor that was like my mom in there.

COVID-19 is real, and it's taking lives. I was lucky because I'm young and healthy. It still did not discriminate. What happened to me may not happen to you, but is it worth the risk? We are the key right now. We are lacking the right kind of leadership during this pandemic so please, take charge of your life and your health to do what is right.

THE ANTI-MASK LEAGUE OF 1918

The need to wear masks is not new. More than one hundred years ago, during the 1918–1919 Spanish flu pandemic, public health authorities, along with mayors of many major cities, urged people to wear masks to reduce the spread of influenza. People generally complied with the order in the spring and summer of 1918. But by fall of 1918, people rebelled against masks, even though the flu had killed 195,000 Americans in October alone. Famous people shunned masks because they wanted the public to recognize them. Others complained about the loss of comfort and freedom. Men poked holes in their masks so they could smoke cigars.

As the pandemic moved into its second year, resistance to masks became stronger. Government officials levied fines on those who failed to wear masks, but it didn't seem to help. A lawyer founded the Anti-Mask League of San Francisco, turning masks into a political symbol rather than a means of slowing a pandemic. Objectors said that forcing people to wear masks was unconstitutional and that there was no scientific evidence they worked. By the end of the pandemic, flu had killed thirty out of every one thousand people in San Francisco, making it one of the hardest-hit cities in the nation.

KEEP YOUR DISTANCE

The coronavirus is most easily spread through respiratory droplets that spew out when an infected person coughs, sneezes, laughs, sings, or even talks loudly. The wet droplets fall to the floor within a few feet. These activities also produce a large number of smaller particles—aerosolized mist, similar to what a can of hair spray puts out. These tiny particles travel 15 feet (4.6 m) or more and can hang in the air for several hours, possibly infecting anyone who walks through them. Both droplets and mist can land in the mouth or noses of nearby people, be inhaled into the lungs, and cause infection.

Early in the pandemic, health authorities warned people to stay 6 feet (2 m) away from one another. Many stores and public places marked the floor with decals or stickers to show how far 6 feet was. But by August 2020, experts sounded the warning that 6 feet may not be enough. Factors such as air circulation, ventilation, exposure time, crowd density, whether people were wearing face masks, and whether they were speaking, shouting, or singing all affected the chances of a person catching the virus.

People without symptoms who don't know they have it can spread the virus. People with no symptoms unknowingly transmit more than half of COVID-19 cases. That's why the CDC called for people to social distance—to limit one's time outside of the home and stay at least 6 feet (2 m) away from others. The strictest form of social distancing was the stay-at-home orders that some governors and mayors imposed on their states and cities. One study showed that stay-at-home orders reduced the infection rate by 58 percent. At the same time, British researchers estimated shutdowns in the UK cut the infection rate there by 82 percent.

Solomon Hsiang, leader of a UC Berkeley research team, said, "Without these policies employed, we would have lived through a very different April and May [2020]. The disease was spreading at a really extraordinary rate that is rare even among very infectious diseases." While acknowledging the difficulty of the shutdown, Hsiang said, "I don't think any human endeavor has ever saved so many lives in such a short period of time. There have been huge personal costs to staying home and canceling events, but the data show that each day made a profound difference. By using science and cooperating, we changed the course of history."

CLEAN HANDS

Viruses such as SARS-CoV-2 can be passed by dirty hands. If infected people touch their mouth, nose, or eyes, and then touch a surface such as a table, a healthy person may possibly become infected by touching the table afterward. Thorough handwashing—for at least twenty seconds—is an excellent way to destroy the virus and prevent infection. And you don't need a special antibacterial soap—any soap will do. Soap latches onto viruses and bacteria and allows them to be flushed down the drain when you rinse your hands. It's particularly tough on the coronavirus. "[Soap] is almost like a demolition team breaking down a building and taking all the bricks away," says chemistry professor Palli Thordarson of the University of New South Wales.

When soap is not available, many stores and offices provide hand sanitizers. When using a sanitizer, spread it all over your hands, including between the fingers, and then rub your hands together vigorously until dry. Most hand sanitizers contain at least 60 percent alcohol, which kills bacteria and viruses on your hands.

ONE STUDY SHOWED THAT BETWEEN MARCH 1 AND AUGUST 1 OF 2020, COVID-19 CAUSED AT LEAST 20 PERCENT MORE DEATHS THAN NORMALLY EXPECTED FROM ALL CAUSES IN THE US.

Although washing hands is important, dirty hands are not the primary way by which SARS-CoV-2 spreads. The CDC announced in May 2020 that most people were not infected with the virus by touching contaminated objects. Many people stopped wiping down their packages, garbage cans, mail, and newspapers, knowing that the risk of getting the virus by touch was lower than first believed. "What we're seeing . . . is that COVID is not spreading heavily through touch," Colin Furness, an epidemiologist at the University of Toronto, said. "It is possible to contract the virus through surfaces, but it's not happening very often."

TESTING FOR COVID-19

Testing people to see if they were infected with SARS-CoV-2 can help flatten the curve by identifying people who may be infected with, or who may have been exposed to, COVID-19. Throughout the SARS-CoV-2 pandemic, doctors told infected people or exposed people to quarantine themselves for a minimum of fourteen days to ensure they didn't spread the disease to others. Only if their symptoms became serious were they to seek care at a hospital. The CDC recommended testing for people with symptoms of COVID-19 and for people who had close contact with someone with COVID-19. Health-care providers often required testing before elective hospital admissions or surgeries. People returning to school or work usually needed testing. Professional sports teams had frequent—often daily—COVID-19 tests because they were in close contact with one another. Some airlines required their passengers be tested before boarding planes. Health-care professionals had to be tested frequently to ensure they had not become infected at their work sites.

Yet COVID-19 tests were often in short supply, with not enough to keep up with the demand. News reports showed people waiting for hours in lines on foot and in cars for a test. Sometimes it took longer for results to become available than for the virus to leave the patient's body. Laboratories had huge backlogs of tests to run because a chemical needed to process the tests was out of stock. Sometimes people died of the disease without being tested or before their results were known. And COVID-19 tests were not perfect. Harvard Hospital found the rate of false negatives, in which the test shows a person doesn't have the virus but they actually do have it, ranged from 0 to 30 percent.

The federal government lacked a plan to provide adequate numbers of tests to states. Many states had to find their own test kits and distribute them. For example, California governor Gavin Newsom contracted with a company in that state to process an additional 150,000 tests per day. The results were available within twenty-four to

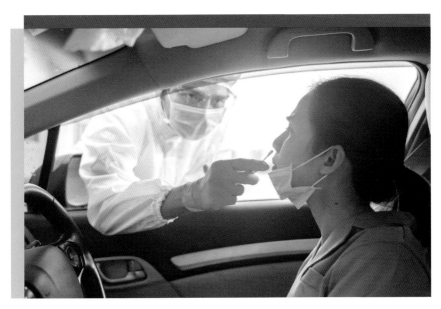

Tests for COVID-19 often involved swabbing the inside of patients' nostrils, producing uncomfortable sensations. Later, researchers developed tests that sampled patients' saliva.

forty-eight hours. During a press conference, Newsom said, "California is using its market power to combat global supply chain challenges and protect Californians in the fight against COVID-19. Supply chains across the country have slowed as demand for COVID-19 tests have increased." In December 2020, the FDA authorized the first at-home testing kit for COVID-19. It didn't require a prescription and cost thirty dollars, making it convenient and accessible for people who could not locate a testing program.

Two kinds of COVID-19 tests each tested for different things. The first was diagnostic testing to show if people had active infections. If so, they needed to isolate themselves from other people and seek medical care as needed. The second type of test was an antibody test that provided evidence of past COVID-19 infections. The immune system produces antibodies in response to a specific disease to fight infections. For example, if you had the measles vaccination when you were a child, your blood has antibodies to fight measles off if you're exposed to it again. Antibodies for COVID-19 show that a person had the disease in the past. In December 2020, a study in *Science* magazine found that antibodies to SARS-CoV-2 infection lasted for a few months, protecting some people—but not all—from reinfection.

CONTACT TRACING

Contact tracing and testing of contacts is another way to flatten the curve. The CDC defines contact as being within 6 feet (2 m) of an infected (or probably infected) person for fifteen minutes or more. Contact tracing uses public health staff to track down anyone who might have been infected by a recently diagnosed person. The contact tracer works with patients to help them remember who they were in contact with just before they became ill. The tracers locate the contacts as soon as possible and tell them that they've been exposed to COVID-19 and that they should stay at home for fourteen days. The tracer tells contacts to maintain social distancing, to check their temperature twice a day, and to watch out for coughing or shortness of breath. If any of these occur, the contacts should isolate themselves and call the tracer back to determine if medical care is necessary. Google, Apple, and some states rolled out smartphone apps that notify you if you've been exposed to COVID-19. To protect people's privacy, the apps do not tell you exactly who tested positive. While this is not true contact tracing, it suggests to people who've been exposed that they may want to be tested.

Amy Driscoll, a recovering coronavirus patient in Ohio, received a call from her county health department two hours after she got home from the hospital in May 2020. She said they had a long list of questions for her. "Who have I seen in the last two weeks? Where was I in the last two weeks? Who was I in contact with? Where do I work?" The contact tracers got in touch with her coworkers, a restaurant where she went for lunch, a hair salon she had visited, and people who

Several cities, states, and countries developed contact-tracing apps that alert the user to any potential exposures to COVID-19. The apps work by monitoring the user's location and communicating with other users' apps. A user who tests positive can report the test results to the app. Then anyone else with the app who had recently been in contact with that user receives an alert for a potential exposure.

sat close to her at a Cleveland Cavaliers game. To protect patient privacy, contacts are only informed they've been exposed to an infected patient and are not told the name of the person who exposed them.

Contact tracing can be effective in slowing the spread of a disease, but the large number of COVID-19 patients makes it challenging. In July 2020, an article in a health-care journal said the US was reporting twenty thousand new COVID-19 cases every day. Each case—or patient—can average more than thirty close contacts. That's six hundred thousand people who should be reached and asked to voluntarily quarantine. The article concludes, "In a country where quarantines are voluntary, the sheer number of people under quarantine combined with the onerous length of the quarantine period may encourage many to simply disregard quarantine recommendations, undermining contact tracing efforts." And allowing the continued spread of SARS-CoV-2.

CHAPTER 7

HEALTH CARE FIGHTS BACK

COVID-19 IS LIKE A BURGLAR WHO SLIPS IN YOUR UNLOCKED SECOND-FLOOR WINDOW AND STARTS TO RANSACK YOUR HOUSE. ONCE INSIDE, THEY DON'T JUST TAKE YOUR STUFF—THEY ALSO THROW OPEN ALL YOUR DOORS AND WINDOWS SO THEIR ACCOMPLICES CAN RUSH IN AND HELP PILLAGE MORE EFFICIENTLY.

—Thomas Smith, journalist, 2020

When cases of COVID-19 began appearing in the US early in 2020, doctors thought the virus only killed the elderly and those with a preexisting disease such as diabetes. They didn't realize some people could have COVID-19 but experience no symptoms. Health-care workers thought the virus attacked only the lungs and didn't know it could affect other organs in the body. They didn't know people would spend weeks attached to ventilators to breathe for them. There was no cure and no specific treatment for COVID-19. Doctors around the world had a lot to learn. By the fall of 2020, COVID-19 was the third-leading cause of death in the United States, surpassed only by heart disease and cancer. COVID-19 completely turned Americans' lives around.

WHO GETS COVID-19?

COVID-19 affects people of all ages, genders, and races, but early on, doctors noticed trends. For example, people of color develop

COVID-19 and die of it more often than white people. People with chronic medical conditions, such as diabetes, heart problems, and kidney disease, were more likely to develop severe cases of COVID-19. Obesity was also a predictor of how sick a person may become. One major study from August 2020 found that obese people who come down with COVID-19 were twice as likely to be hospitalized, far more likely to be admitted to an ICU, and more likely to die. Nearly 38 percent of American adults and 21 percent of teens are obese, putting them at greater risk for COVID-19 and its complications.

Another unexpected finding was how gender affects COVID-19. Men were nearly twice as likely to become severely ill and to die as were women, regardless of age. This was true in most countries that kept accurate statistics on COVID-19 cases. One reason might be that women tend to produce far more T-cells than do men. T-cells are white blood cells that are part of the immune system. They quickly respond to infections such as COVID-19 and find and destroy infected cells to keep the virus from spreading. The T-cell response of most ninety-year-old women is as strong as that of forty-year-old men.

Age is a well-known risk factor for severe illness and death from COVID-19. Older people are more likely to have underlying medical conditions and weakened immune systems than younger people. While younger people seldom got as sick with COVID-19 as older people, they were more likely to catch it. In the fall of 2020, the CDC reported that twenty- to twenty-nine-year-olds accounted for nearly one-fourth of new infections, the highest of any group. The average age for all

EARLY IN THE PANDEMIC, DOCTORS FACED BIZARRE COMPLICATIONS IN CRITICALLY ILL PATIENTS. "WE WERE FLYING BLIND. THERE IS NOTHING MORE DISTURBING FOR ME AS A DOCTOR."

—Dr. Jose Pascual, University of Pennsylvania Health System, 2020.

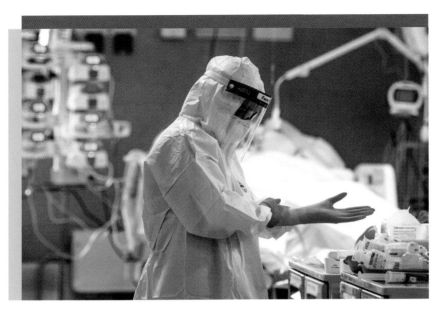

Hospital workers had to wear full personal protective equipment (often abbreviated to PPE) when treating people during the pandemic. Some hospitals struggled to provide PPE for all their workers at times due to supply shortages and lack of government assistance.

cases of COVID-19 cases declined from forty-six years old in May to thirty-eight years old in just a few months.

Sometimes younger people underestimate the risk of certain activities and are more likely to take risks than older people. "It feels like my youth is being stolen from me," twenty-three-year old Branko Zlatar told a newspaper reporter when explaining why he chose to go out during the pandemic. "That is why people my age ignore it. I don't want to waste time indoors when I should be out living life." After meeting at a bar with friends in the summer of 2020, Zlatar became ill.

RESEARCHERS FOUND THAT PEOPLE WITH TYPE O BLOOD—THE MOST COMMON BLOOD TYPE IN THE US—MAY BE LESS LIKELY TO GET COVID AND LESS LIKELY TO BECOME SEVERELY ILL.

THE NOSE KNOWS

Dogs' sense of smell is so good that humans use them to detect bombs and drugs. They can also help out in medical settings by detecting cancer, seizures, and low blood sugar. Is it any surprise they can also sniff out the SARS-CoV-2 virus? Researchers are testing the ability of dogs to smell coronavirus in samples from infected patients and healthy patients. The dogs are correct more than 95 percent of the time. Some airlines offer rapid COVID-19 tests before boarding for a safer flight. A dog could screen 250 people in an hour—far more quickly than any COVID-19 test. Finland's Helsinki airport uses ten dogs trained to detect the disease, and they are nearly 100 percent accurate. Other airports around the world are training dogs to detect COVID-19. Isn't it nicer to be sniffed by a dog than to wait for a COVID-19 test?

He had a test for the virus, but continued to see his friends while waiting for the results. It turned out that Zlatar had COVID-19 and a close friend of his got it as well. He quickly changed his tune after his diagnosis, saying, "I want people to know it [COVID-19] is real. A lot of people don't take it seriously." Zlatar admitted feeling guilty, and after he recovered, he donated his plasma to be used to treat others with COVID-19.

INFECTED BUT NOT SICK

As the pandemic raged on, researchers began to notice that at least four out of ten people who tested positive for COVID-19 had no symptoms. People infected with SARS-CoV-2 but who do not have symptoms accounted for at least one-half of all virus transmissions. Why doesn't everyone feel sick when they're infected? Studies suggested a couple of reasons for this surprising finding.

Some people's symptoms were so mild they never guessed they had COVID-19. They may have admitted to "feeling out of sorts" with headaches, trouble sleeping, a tickle in the throat, or mild nausea and diarrhea.

The amount of viruses you receive likely determines how sick you get. For example, if an infected person sneezes into your face, you'll receive far more viruses than if they sneezed from across the room while wearing a mask, and you'll probably get sicker.

Initially, doctors believed no one in the world had any immunity to SARS-CoV-2, but that was not entirely accurate. Of the seven coronaviruses known to infect people, four cause mild respiratory infections and sometimes pneumonia. The other three, SARS-CoV-1, MERS-CoV, and SARS-CoV-2, can cause serious illness. By fall of 2020, evidence suggested that having had one of the four milder coronaviruses may provide partial immunity to the SARS-CoV-2 virus. T-cells, which recognize previous infections and help fight them off, may also recognize the new virus as a coronavirus and provide some degree of immunity. One group of studies showed that 50 percent of blood drawn in the US between 2015 and 2018 (before SARS-CoV-2 struck) showed T-cells that seemed to "recognize" SARS-CoV-2. Similar findings were found in several European countries, suggesting partial immunity to SARS-CoV-2 could be more widespread than expected.

SYMPTOMS OF COVID-19 AND LASTING PROBLEMS

While some people infected with SARS-CoV-2 have few, if any, symptoms, the majority will know they're sick. Symptoms of the disease it causes, COVID-19, are similar to those of the flu and include fatigue, shortness of breath or difficulty breathing, cough, muscle aches, chills, sore throat, headache, rash, nausea, vomiting, and diarrhea. The sudden loss of taste and smell is unique to COVID-19.

Symptoms should be evaluated by a health-care professional to determine if hospitalization is needed.

As the pandemic progressed month after month, doctors began to realize the virus could affect nearly every part of the body: lungs, heart, liver, kidneys, brain, and immune system. And some people were sick for many months. They learned that even some people who had no symptoms could be left with heart problems.

COVID-19 hit actor Alyssa Milano hard. "I had never been this kind of sick. Everything hurt. Loss of smell. It felt like an elephant was sitting on my chest. I couldn't breathe. I couldn't keep food in me. I lost nine pounds [4 kg] in two weeks. I was confused. Low grade fever. And the headaches were horrible. I basically had every [COVID-19] symptom." She felt dizzy, was short of breath, had memory loss, and experienced irregular heartbeats. "This illness is not a hoax. I thought I was dying. It felt like I was dying. Please take care of yourselves. Please wash your hands and wear a mask and social distance. I don't want anyone to feel the way I felt. Be well." Milano got sick in April 2020 and still experienced symptoms months later, making her a long-hauler, a person whose COVID-19 symptoms last over many months.

Like most viruses, SARS-CoV-2 is so tiny that one thousand viruses would have to line up to equal the width of a human hair. Yet once the virus enters the body through the eyes, nose, or mouth, it can take over many organs. First, the virus attacks cells in the nose, reproducing and spreading down the airway to the lungs. People may notice a cough, a fever, headache, or a sore throat. Flu and colds typically infect only the upper airway, but SARS-CoV-2 infects the entire respiratory system, from the nose to the millions of tiny air sacs in the lungs called alveoli. The alveoli exchange the oxygen you inhale for the carbon dioxide you exhale, ensuring your body has all the oxygen it needs. This explains why shortness of breath and a feeling of not getting enough air are early signs of COVID-19.

Symptoms of COVID-19

 Lungs: clogging and inflammation of alveoli, difficulty breathing, pulmonary embolism due to blood clots

 Heart: weakening of heart muscle; arrhythmia and heart attacks due to blood clots

 Nose: loss of smell and taste

 Gastrointestinal system: diarrhea, vomiting

 Immune system: overactive immune response that attacks healthy tissue

 Kidneys: damaging of blood filtration structures

 Eyes: pink eye

 Blood: blood clots; attacks on the lining of the blood vessels

 Skin: rashes on toes or fingers due to attacks on blood vessels

 Brain: stroke due to blood clots, neurological issues

COVID-19 affects many parts of the body. People could experience some or all of these symptoms.

In severe cases, dead cells and fluid fill the lungs. The damage can be so bad that a few people have required lung transplants to survive.

SARS-CoV-2 frequently attacks the kidneys. Early in the pandemic, doctors were startled to find that for every ten COVID-19 patients who were sick enough to be in intensive care units, as many as three had lost kidney function. They required dialysis, which cleans the blood when the kidneys cannot. Dr. Alan Kliger, a kidney specialist at Yale University School of Medicine, said, "That's a huge number of people who have this problem. That's new to me. I think it's very possible that the virus attaches to the kidney cells and attacks them."

As 2020 progressed, doctors discovered that many patients—even those with mild cases of COVID-19—may experience damage to the heart and blood vessels. One study looked at the hearts of one hundred people who had recovered from COVID-19. Researchers found that seventy-eight of them had evidence of heart damage similar to that of a heart attack, and sixty had signs of inflammation, signaling an overactive immune response to infection. Cardiologist Dr. Valentina Puntmann, who led the study, said, "The fact that 78 percent of 'recovered' [patients] had evidence of ongoing heart involvement means

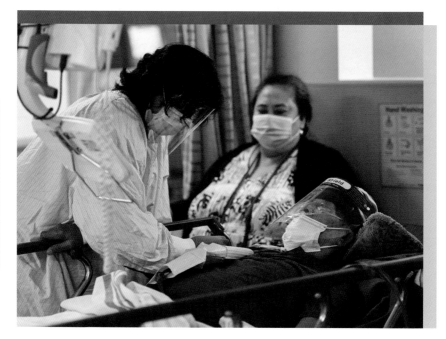

An elderly man receives dialysis as part of his treatment for COVID-19.

that the heart is involved in a majority of patients, even if COVID-19 illness does not scream out with the classical heart symptoms, such as chest pain." These conditions could seriously affect the heart's ability to pump blood to the body and ultimately result in heart failure.

COVID-19 can also lead to the formation of blood clots in all the blood vessels of the body. Blood clots often begin in the legs and travel upward. They might reach the lungs and cause the patient to stop breathing. Clots might also reach the heart and cause heart attacks. Or clots can bypass the lungs and heart and travel to the brain. In April 2020 in New York City, then the epicenter of the pandemic, doctors noticed a large number of patients coming into the emergency room with strokes. A stroke occurs when a blood clot travels to the brain, where it can damage parts of the brain that control speech and movement. The patients had the very serious strokes typically found in older people that leave them paralyzed on one side of the body. But these patients were in their thirties and forties. Some blood clots that reach the brain don't cause strokes. Instead, they may cause confusion, dementia, psychosis, and inflammation of the brain. Clots also caused the newly identified foot problem COVID toes, in which toes become painful, discolored, and swollen.

College student Bethany Nesbitt suddenly died of a blood clot to the lungs in her Indiana dorm in early November 2020. She'd been sick for a few days and quarantined in her room. Her brother Stephen Nesbitt, tweeted, "Our hearts are shattered. My sweet sister, Bethany, died as she slept in her dorm room Thursday night. She was 20. She was COVID-19 positive. The cause of death was a pulmonary embolism—the result of a blood clot—widely recognized as a common cause of death in COVID-19 patients."

Doctors realized that COVID-19 is far more unpredictable than a simple respiratory virus such as influenza. "We don't know why there are so many disease presentations," said Angela Rasmussen, virologist at Columbia University's Mailman School of Public Health. "Bottom

FIVE COMMON CORONAVIRUS MYTHS

MYTH 1: Only older people get sick. Not true.

REASON? People of any age can get COVID-19, especially if they have preexisting medical conditions.

MYTH 2: Masks can't protect you against COVID-19. Not true.

REASON? Wearing a good surgical or cloth mask can reduce the risk of getting the disease by 56 percent.

MYTH 3: You can only catch COVID-19 if you've been in close contact with someone who has symptoms. Not true.

REASON? People who are infected but have few, if any, symptoms can pass COVID-19 on to other people.

MYTH 4: COVID-19 is like the flu. Not true.

REASON? COVID-19 is much more serious than flu. By fall of 2020, it was the third-leading cause of death in Americans, after cancer and heart disease.

MYTH 5: Everyone can get vaccinated against COVID-19 as soon as a vaccine becomes available. Not true.

REASON? States will provide vaccinations to the people most at risk before offering them to everyone who wants one.

line, this is just so new that there's a lot we don't know." As doctors struggled to recognize the many symptoms of the new coronavirus, they also scrambled for ways to treat patients.

TREATING COVID-19

According to the CDC, about eight out of ten people with COVID-19 had mild to moderate symptoms and recovered at home. Few specific treatments for COVID-19 were used in the early months of the pandemic. Some of the things that help people with the flu feel better also helped with COVID-19. These include getting enough rest, drinking plenty of fluids, and taking medications for fever and aches. These steps relieve symptoms while the body's immune system fights off the virus.

However, the other two out of ten people with COVID-19 developed severe symptoms and required hospitalization. In these situations, hospitalized patients were given supportive care, including receiving fluids intravenously to keep them hydrated. Patients who could not eat were likely to be fed through a tube that went into the stomach or with special intravenous fluids that supplied much of the nutrition that food provides.

Most hospitalized COVID-19 patients needed oxygen. Early in the pandemic, doctors noted many of these patients had very low levels of oxygen in the body. Doctors often sedated and intubated these patients and put them on ventilators to increase oxygen levels. Intubation is when a doctor inserts a breathing tube through the nose or throat and threads it down the trachea and into the lungs. The tube is connected to a ventilator. The machine sends a steady supply of oxygen under pressure into the patient's lungs. While this rapidly improves oxygenation, it's risky because it requires heavy sedation for long periods.

When possible, doctors opted for less invasive methods to deliver oxygen. This included oxygen delivered by nasal cannulas—small plastic tabs that go into the nostrils. Patients also received oxygen with masks fitted over their mouths and noses or with pressurized hoods that fit over the patient's entire head. The hoods often worked as well as intubation, were easier for the patient to tolerate, and helped reduce hospital staff workload. Sometimes, hospital staff positioned patients in a prone position—face down on their stomachs—with good results. This position reduced the pressure of the heart and diaphragm on the lungs.

As with many illnesses, doctors also gave patients medications to treat COVID-19 symptoms. Some of the medications had been used for years, while others were new, experimental, or in clinical trials to learn if they are safe and effective. Doctors sometimes administered

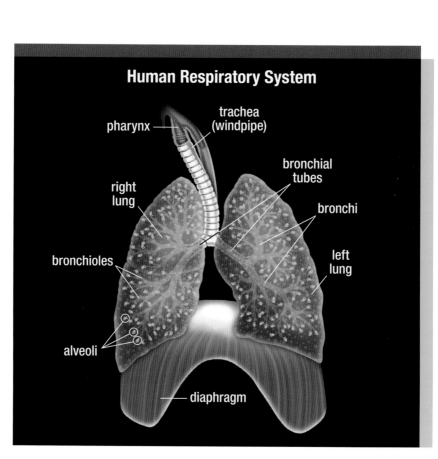

Human Respiratory System

pharynx

trachea (windpipe)

bronchial tubes

right lung

bronchi

bronchioles

left lung

alveoli

diaphragm

This diagram depicts a healthy human respiratory system. COVID-19 attacks the alveoli, causing inflammation and fluids to build in the lungs. Clots can also form in the blood vessels that normally take oxygen from the lungs and distribute it to the rest of the body.

blood thinners such as heparin to help prevent the blood clots so common with COVID-19 patients. Heparin reduced the risk of death by nearly one-half when given to seriously ill patients.

The steroid dexamethasone helps prevent inflammation. It's used for many medical conditions, from a painful sprained ankle to cancer. Physicians used it on critically ill COVID-19 patients to help control inflammation and to inhibit an overactive immune system. Sometimes when fighting a viral infection, immune systems go into overdrive, which does more harm than good in severe cases. One study showed giving steroids to the sickest COVID-19 patients reduced their risk of death by 34 percent, compared with patients who did not receive them.

For years, doctors have given patients convalescent plasma to help treat other viral diseases such as hepatitis and Ebola. Plasma is the liquid part of blood that remains when red blood cells are removed. People who had recently recovered from COVID-19 had high levels of antibodies in their blood, produced by their immune system as they fought the disease. Researchers thought COVID-19 antibodies in the recovered patient's plasma might help defeat the virus in sick patients. Convalescent plasma seemed to work in some COVID-19 patients who were in clinical studies. In August 2020, the FDA approved its use in an Emergency Use Authorization. Then convalescent plasma could be used in a hospitalized patient for COVID-19 when no other treatment was available. However, the plasma actually had little effect on patients who were already sick enough to be in a hospital. More recent studies showed the plasma reduced the risk of developing a severe case of COVID-19 by 48 percent among patients who received it within three days of diagnosis. While that's good news for the treatment of COVID-19, few people were receiving medical care that soon after diagnosis because they hadn't yet developed symptoms.

While antiviral medications are used to treat several diseases, they aren't cures. Instead, they slow the production of new viruses in cells, shortening the duration of illness and decreasing complications. The antiviral drug remdesivir was originally developed by pharmaceutical company Gilead Sciences to fight hepatitis. It targets a part of the virus that makes an enzyme it needs to replicate. The medication effectively treated both SARS-CoV-1 and MERS-CoV patients. A study published in the *New England Journal of Medicine* showed the recovery time for patients with COVID-19 who received remdesivir was eleven days, versus fifteen days without it. In October 2020, the FDA approved remdesivir as a treatment for patients with severe

COVID-19. Dr. Stephen M. Hahn, then FDA commissioner, said, "The FDA is committed to expediting the development and availability of COVID-19 treatments during this unprecedented public health emergency . . . the agency will continue to help move new medical products to patients as soon as possible, while at the same time determining whether they are effective and if their benefits outweigh their risks." This was the first official approval of a treatment for COVID-19.

The medication famotidine is commonly used to reduce heartburn but is also used to treat COVID-19. A review of the medical records for more than six thousand people showed the death rate from COVID-19 was 13 percent lower for those who took famotidine. "The active ingredient for the over-the-counter heartburn medication is being tested as a treatment for COVID-19, only at nine times the dosage and administered intravenously," according to Dr. Chauncey Crandall of Palm Beach Cardiovascular Clinic. As of the winter of 2020, the medication was in a clinical trial involving hospitalized patients with moderate to severe COVID-19. Researchers believe famotidine may bind to a viral enzyme and hinder the virus's replication.

Regeneron is a large drug company that developed an antibody "cocktail" to help COVID-19 patients. Crandall describes it this way. "First, [Regeneron] scientists have isolated antibodies from humans who have recovered from COVID-19. Second, Regeneron also genetically altered mice that have humanlike immune systems [and then exposed them to] SARS-CoV-2 with the goal of . . . creating antibodies to fight COVID-19." This antibody cocktail could function both as a preventive vaccine and as a treatment. However, it's difficult to produce and is very expensive. When given early in the illness to patients not yet hospitalized, the antibody cocktail reduced hospitalizations and ER visits. Clinical trials are underway to determine its effectiveness for COVID-19. A few people have received the medication under the FDA's Emergency Use Authorization rule.

CLINICAL TRIALS

Clinical trials investigate how new medications work. All prescription medications and vaccines go through clinical trials before the FDA approves them for use. People volunteer to participate in clinical trials, which have these four phases:

- **PHASE 1.** Is the medication safe? The drug is given for the first time to a small number of healthy people to determine its safety, dosage, and side effects.

- **PHASE 2.** Does the medication work? A larger group of people receive the drug to determine if it is both safe and effective for the condition it's intended to treat.

- **PHASE 3.** How does the new medication compare with existing medications? Thousands of people take the drug to confirm its effectiveness, to monitor side effects, and to compare it with other medications to treat the same condition and with placebos (fake medications that have no effect). These studies are randomized and double-blinded—neither the patient nor the researcher know who received the medication and who received a placebo.

- **PHASE 4.** This phase may involve millions of people taking the drug for years to identify any long-term side effects. During this time, doctors are allowed to use the medication for other purposes than the one for which it was originally intended.

Researchers are studying many other medications as possible treatments for COVID-19. These include interferon to ramp up the body's own immune system, interleukin to help control an overactive immune system, and antiviral drugs currently used to treat HIV. The FDA also approved several monoclonal antibody drugs. These are laboratory-developed antibodies that bind to viruses and keep them from replicating.

By late 2020, outcomes had improved for COVID-19 patients. Patients in one study had a one-in-four chance of dying at the start of the pandemic. Nine months later, the chance of dying was less than one in ten. The improvement was due to several factors. Increased mask wearing meant patients inhaled a smaller amount of the virus and were therefore not as ill. Fewer patients were being intubated and put on

ONE NURSE'S STORY

Simone Hannah-Clark is a nurse who worked in a New York City hospital intensive care unit during the pandemic. She wrote a piece for the *New York Times* about one of her days. "My first task is to help with post-mortem care on a COVID-19 patient we just lost," she said. "We had watched her slowly die over the past few days. We did everything we could. It's just me and a nursing colleague in the room. It's a grim affair. We wrap the patient's body securely, stroking her brow and wishing her well on her next journey. My colleague removes her jewelry carefully; we know her daughter will want it. I have to collect her belongings because security isn't allowed to come into the room. It moves me to see her wallet, her planner, her toiletries. Only a week ago she was a person with a future, with plans, with cherry-flavored lip balm."

ventilators. Doctors more readily recognized the danger of body-wide blood clots and signs of an overactive immune response. Standardized treatments became the norm.

WHEN A PRESIDENT PRESCRIBES

Health-care experts didn't know much about how to treat COVID-19 at the start of the pandemic. Sometimes their recommendations contradicted one another or they changed course two weeks later. That wasn't a surprise. SARS-CoV-2 was new, and there was no handbook on how to treat it. One thing experts had in common was that they followed the science—at least the science as it was known at the time—in making their recommendations about patient care.

However, throughout much of 2020, suggestions for the treatment of COVID-19 poured out of the Trump White House. These ideas were not based on science. Instead, they came from rumors and, in some cases, may have benefited major donors to the president's political campaign.

Chloroquine and hydroxychloroquine have been used for decades to treat malaria, a disease caused by a tiny parasite that mosquitoes carry. In February 2020 Trump attended a fundraiser sponsored by Oracle chairman Larry Ellison, a billionaire technology leader. Five officials in the Trump administration told the *New York Times* that Ellison provided software to the White House "to promote unproven coronavirus treatments, including a pair of malaria drugs publicized by President Trump, potentially before the government approves their use for the outbreak."

For weeks Trump talked about hydroxychloroquine and chloroquine in interviews and on Twitter. He felt the FDA should approve it as a cure, calling it a "game changer" and saying, "We're going to be able to make that drug available almost immediately."

Chloroquine, however, can cause heart problems and can damage the kidneys and liver. Doctors no longer use either of these medications to treat malaria because of side effects and because parasites that cause malaria are resistant to them. Dr. Rick Bright, a top official with the US Health and Human Services, lost his job when he disagreed with the White House about funding potentially dangerous drugs promoted by people with political connections.

A medical journal said, "Hydroxychloroquine has been used as a desperate attempt for prophylaxis [prevention] and treatment of COVID-19. The drug has wide-ranging drug interactions and potential cardiotoxicity [heart damage]. Indiscriminate unsupervised use can expose the public to serious adverse drug effects."

In spite of such warnings, Trump took hydroxychloroquine and said he felt fine. He was lucky. In March 2020, an Arizona woman was hospitalized and her husband died after they took chloroquine phosphate, a substance used to clean fish tanks that she used in her own fishpond. The woman said they took it after seeing Trump discuss it on television. "Trump kept saying it was basically pretty much a cure."

After Trump attended a White House briefing in April 2020 that mentioned how effective disinfectants such as hand sanitizers are at killing the virus, he said, "I see the disinfectant that knocks it out in a minute, one minute. Is there a way we can do something like that by injection inside, or almost a cleaning? Because you see it gets inside the lungs and it does a tremendous number on the lungs, so it would be interesting to check that."

Disinfectants can be poisonous if consumed. Poison control centers reported a spike in calls about drinking disinfectants to prevent COVID-19. Across the nation people swallowed, gargled, or washed their sinuses out with bleach, disinfectants, and alcohol, often suffering serious injury. The CDC reported at least fifteen cases in which people drank hand sanitizers. Four died and others experienced seizures and vision loss. "Words have consequences," emergency room physician Robert Glatter wrote about Trump's comments.

At a press conference in April 2020, President Donald Trump asked if disinfectants can be consumed or injected to fight against the coronavirus.

At the same briefing where disinfectants were discussed, a Trump official mentioned a study underway about how environmental factors such as sunlight affected the virus on surfaces or in the air. Taking it a step further, Trump said, "So, supposing we hit the body with a tremendous—whether it's ultraviolet or just very powerful light—and I think you said that hasn't been checked but you're going to test it. And then I said, supposing you brought the light inside of the body, which you can do either through the skin or in some other way." These are not recognized treatments for COVID-19.

In August 2020, Michael Lindell, founder of a pillow company and a major financial supporter of Trump, promoted oleandrin, made from the oleander plant, as a cure for COVID-19. Oleander plants are some of the most poisonous plants in the world, and while some traditional medicine practices use oleandrin to treat heart-related issues, it is not a sufficient treatment for COVID-19. Trump immediately wanted the FDA to approve it without testing it. Online searches for "buy oleandrin" spiked on Google, as some people considered using it.

Cassandra Quave, medical ethnobotanist at Atlanta's Emory University, said, "There are more than 100 studies in the scientific and medical literature reporting the deaths of both humans and livestock following consumption of the oleander plant, and oleandrin is the main chemical component of the plant. . . . The dangers of oleander . . . are well-known from years of prior studies by many different scientific and medical teams."

Trump's misstatements, incorrect assumptions, and his willingness to bypass established scientific protocol for the approval of new drugs put many people in danger. They also forced scientists to spend valuable time trying to correct an uninformed president—time that could have been better spent tending patients or conducting scientific studies.

CDC LEADERS SPEAK OUT

In July 2020, four former directors of the world-renowned Centers for Disease Control and Prevention collaborated on an article for the *Washington Post*. They said, "We ran the CDC. No president ever politicized its science the way Trump has." Drs. Tom Frieden, Jeffrey Koplan, David Satcher, and Richard Besser opened the article by saying:

> The four of us led the CDC over a period of more than 15 years, spanning Republican and Democratic administrations alike. We cannot recall over our collective tenure a single time when political pressure led to a change in the interpretation of scientific evidence. The CDC is home to thousands of experts who for decades have fought deadly pathogens such as HIV, Zika, and Ebola. . . . These are the people best positioned to help our country emerge

from this crisis as safely as possible. Unfortunately, their sound science is being challenged with partisan potshots, sowing confusion and mistrust at a time when the American people need leadership, expertise and clarity. These efforts have even fueled a backlash against public health officials across the country: Public servants have been harassed, threatened, and forced to resign when we need them most. This is unconscionable and dangerous.

These experts go on to say that disregard for public health guidelines led to a sharp rise in infections and death. "America now stands as a global outlier in the coronavirus pandemic. The United States now has more cases and deaths than any other country." This is what can happen when one of the wealthiest nations in the world lacks a comprehensive pandemic policy.

CHAPTER 8
THE WINTER SURGE

WITHOUT A CORONAVIRUS VACCINE, WE WILL NEVER BE ABLE TO LIVE NORMALLY AGAIN. THE ONLY REAL EXIT STRATEGY FROM THIS CRISIS IS A VACCINE THAT CAN BE ROLLED OUT WORLDWIDE.

—Dr. Peter Piot, virologist and director at the London School of Hygiene & Tropical Medicine, 2020

After a brief period when COVID-19 cases seemed to have stabilized, case counts began to rise sharply during the late fall and winter of 2020. Experts had predicted this third wave of cases—the winter surge—would occur as weather grew colder around the nation and people stayed indoors more often. That forced people to be in much closer contact and increased the risk of getting COVID-19. An even bigger contributor to higher case counts were the holidays. Beginning with Thanksgiving and on through the winter holidays, people traveled more than they had since the pandemic began. Health experts, including Fauci, urged people to stay at home for just a few more months. Exhausted hospital workers joined in the pleas to curtail holiday travel. Millions traveled anyway to spend time with family and friends.

MISERY

The third wave of COVID-19 hit most states in the late fall, through the winter of 2020, and into 2021, driving cases to record highs. That meant more cases, more hospitalizations, and more intensive care beds overflowing with very sick people. The US fell behind most other countries in combating the virus. While several European countries also experienced an early winter surge, they managed to quickly bring it under control. Although the US has only 4.25 percent of the world's population, by mid-January 2021 it had nearly 25 percent of the world's cases of COVID-19. Most of the world's well-off nations did a much better job of controlling COVID than the US did.

German Lopez, senior health journalist for Vox, wrote that the outbreaks "are the result of the public and the country's leaders never taking the virus seriously enough and . . . letting their guard down prematurely. States, with the support of President Donald Trump, moved to reopen. . . . The public embraced the reopenings, going out and often not adhering to recommended precautions like physical distancing and wearing a mask. It's this mix of government withdrawal and public complacency that experts have cited in explaining why states continue to struggle with getting the coronavirus under control."

Daily case counts skyrocketed. People skeptical of the worsening pandemic pointed out that many more people were being tested for COVID-19 than in the past. That was true. Office workers, students, teachers, and athletes were tested frequently, sometimes every few days. But the case rate represents the positivity rate—the percentage of those tested who were positive. Positivity rates ranged from 58.8 percent in Idaho to 39 percent in Pennsylvania to 8.7 percent in Minnesota. The higher the positivity rate is, the greater the number of people with COVID-19. By late January, more than one in every 820 Americans had died from COVID-19. And by early spring, 2021, COVID-19 had killed well over half a million Americans. That's more than the number of Americans who died in World War II (1939–1945), the

BY MID-JANUARY 2021, DAILY DEATHS FROM COVID-19 IN THE US TOPPED 4,000. IT TOOK NINETY DAYS FOR THE US TO REACH 2 MILLION CASES OF COVID-19 IN 2020. THE CASE COUNT REACHED 29 MILLION BY THE BEGINNING OF MARCH 2021.

Vietnam War (1954–1957), and the Korean War (1950–1953) combined. By mid-February 2021, the COVID-19 case count exceeded 28 million. The actual number of infected people could have been higher because people with mild symptoms often didn't seek diagnosis.

With the huge increase in COVID-19 cases came very high rates of hospitalizations and admissions to ICUs. By early January 2021, US hospitals held nearly 131,000 COVID-19 patients. ICU beds in some towns and cities were filled. The very sickest COVID-19 patients require the level of care that can only be provided by ICU staff. California adjusted the level of shutdown according to the availability of ICU beds: the fewer ICU beds available in an area, the tighter the restrictions. Across the country, hospitals were overwhelmed, with exhausted staff working long hours in extremely difficult conditions. Patients died without seeing their families, except perhaps on a phone or laptop. If they were lucky, a nurse was with them when they died. It seemed that much of the nation's health-care system was in imminent danger of being totally overwhelmed.

How much worse could things get? Patients with heart attacks, strokes, or in severe auto accidents had trouble receiving emergency care. Ambulances in Los Angeles often waited in line for up to eight hours to deliver their patients to hospitals because there was no room for them. Hospitals across the nation talked about rationing care, limiting it to the people who had the greatest chance of survival. Emergency medical technicians (EMTs) were told that patients who could not be revived at home after their heart stopped beating should not be brought to a hospital. In some cities, EMTs delivered hands-on care in ICUs alongside trained nurses and physicians. Refrigerated trucks held dead bodies in parking lots because hospital morgues had run out of space. Hospitals and paramedics were running short of lifesaving oxygen. And by January, a new mutation of SARS-CoV-2 was circulating in several states and countries. While the mutation seemed more contagious, it did not appear to cause a more serious illness than COVID-19.

The US economy suffered far more during the winter surge than during the previous months. Businesses that had recently reopened were forced to close again. Restaurants could no longer offer outdoor dining but could only provide food to go or for delivery. Job losses climbed, and unemployment benefits were due to expire. After

THE EMOTIONAL TOLL

Catie Carrigan is a twenty-eight-year-old nurse who works in an ICU in Mississippi. In December 2020, she told a *Washington Post* reporter:

> There are some [COVID-19] patients who have been in their younger 20s and their younger 30s, and I think maybe those are the hardest cases. They have families and they have kids just like I do, and it's hard coming into work and taking care of them. Knowing they're supposed to be going to college, they're supposed to be getting married, they're supposed to be having kids and, instead, they're lying in a hospital bed on a ventilator fighting for their life. They have their whole entire lives ahead of them, and then they get hit with this disease that everybody thinks is a hoax and then they die.

months of negotiation, Congress approved a new stimulus package just before leaving Washington, DC, for winter break. It wasn't as generous as the package authorized at the beginning of the pandemic. However, it included $600 for individuals (depending on their income) and a $300-per-week unemployment payment, granted funds to small businesses, and gave money for food, rental assistance, and vaccine distribution.

HOPE

In December 2020, good news about vaccines offered hope during the midst of misery. Vaccines—medications to protect against getting a specific disease—have been around more than two hundred years. In 1796 British surgeon Edward Jenner rubbed cowpox pus into a scrape on an eight-year-old boy's arm. People caught cowpox, a mild disease similar to smallpox, from milking cows. Remarkably, people who had cowpox seldom got smallpox. Jenner later injected the boy with smallpox, and he did not get ill from it. Two years later, the first smallpox vaccine was developed. Over the next 150 years, scientists developed vaccines for anthrax, tetanus, bubonic plague, influenza, and many other serious and deadly diseases that had sickened and killed millions of people for centuries.

Some vaccines took a long time to develop, such as the polio vaccine, which took twenty years. A vaccine to prevent COVID-19 was ready in a fraction of that time because governments around the world supported intensive measures to develop one as quickly as possible. Scientists had been working on dozens of vaccines for COVID-19 since early 2020. Thirty-eight were evaluated in clinical trials in the United States, Europe, and China. Those tested in the US were part of Operation Warp Speed, a partnership among organizations including the CDC, National Institutes of Health (NIH), the Department of Defense, and others. Operation Warp Speed's goal was to produce and deliver millions of doses of safe and effective vaccines.

Organizers of Operation Warp Speed said it could reach that goal by speeding up the development and delivery of a vaccine to prevent COVID-19 while adhering to standards for safety and efficacy. "The speed [of the COVID-19 vaccine] is a reflection of years of work that went before," Fauci said. "That's what the public has to understand." How could a vaccine be developed so quickly?

- Governments around the world financed development of the COVID-19 vaccine with unprecedented amounts of money.
- Scientists didn't start from ground zero. They'd learned a lot about coronaviruses from SARS-CoV-1 and MERS-CoV, so SARS-CoV-2 was somewhat familiar.
- A global outbreak of Ebola virus disease in 2014 to 2016 killed more than ten thousand people. Some governments had developed a pandemic plan for whatever the next global disease would be.
- Chinese scientists discovered the genetic code for SARS-CoV-2 late in 2019 and shared it with the world in January 2020.
- Perhaps most important, scientists discovered in the past few years how to use part of the genetic code of a virus to stimulate a person's immune system to make antibodies to fight it. This method results in developing a new vaccine in record time.

Some people worried that a vaccine created so quickly might result in hurried shortcuts. Early in the pandemic nearly three-fourths of Americans said they would get the vaccine when it was available, but by December—just as the vaccines were rolling out—that number fell to one-half. People feared vaccines had been developed too rapidly to actually work. For those people, the US Department of Health and Human Services explained why the new vaccines would be safe. Phases 1 and 2 of the clinical trials that confirm safety and efficacy were aligned so that trials could proceed more quickly. The government

VACCINE CONSPIRACY THEORIES

With a new vaccine on the way came new conspiracy theories about the perceived dangers of a COVID-19 vaccination. A Pew Research survey said that 71 percent of Americans had heard the COVID-19 outbreak was intentionally planned by people in power. One-third of people who knew of the rumor said it was definitely or probably true. It wasn't. NPR said, "One version of this theory goes something like this: The COVID-19 pandemic is part of a strategy conceived by global elites—such as Bill Gates—to roll out vaccinations with tracking chips that would later be activated by 5G, the new technology for cellular networks."

Kate Starbird of the University of Washington, who studies conspiracy theories, cites one belief: "A rich person controls the world and they want to do bad things so they can continue. . . . Sometimes it's [billionaire] George Soros. Now it's Bill Gates."

oversaw the trials, as opposed to the traditional method, in which pharmaceutical companies decide on their own protocols. Steps such as manufacturing of the vaccine occurred along with clinical trials. No risky shortcuts were allowed during vaccine development. Hahn said at a September Senate hearing, "The FDA will not authorize or approve a vaccine we won't be confident in giving to our families."

The US government, which invested nearly $11 billion in Operation Warp Speed, said the vaccine would be available to everyone and would be free or cost very little. By late fall of 2020, four drug companies, backed in part by US funding, had vaccines in stage 3 clinical trials. The investment paid off.

The American drug company Pfizer, with its German partner, BioNTech, was the first company to gain FDA approval for its

COVID-19 vaccine. After two doses of the vaccine, it appeared to be about 95 percent effective at preventing COVID-19. The downside of the vaccine is that it required storage at extremely low temperatures. New York intensive care nurse Sandra Lindsay received the first COVID-19 vaccine in the US on December 14, 2020, on television. She wanted to reassure other Black people—many of whom mistrust vaccines—that the vaccine was safe. "That was the goal today," she said. "Not to be the first one to take the vaccine, but to inspire people who look like me, who are skeptical in general about taking vaccines."

Another vaccine, developed by Moderna, also requires two doses. It appeared to be nearly 95 percent effective. However, it did not require special handling and shipping like the Pfizer vaccine. Moderna began distribution in late December after FDA approval. AstraZeneca and Oxford University in England worked together on still another vaccine that requires two doses. It appeared to be about 90 percent effective. A single-dose vaccine with an efficacy rate of about 66 percent was developed by Johnson and Johnson and gained FDA approval on February 27, 2021. The fact that it requires only one injection makes this vaccine appealing to people who really dislike getting shots. A single dose is also more convenient to distribute to rural areas and to homeless populations.

The vaccines began being administered before they had been tested in children, teens, pregnant women, and nursing mothers. It was also unclear if people who received a placebo injection during clinical trials should receive the vaccines, and if it would skew long-term results if

Researchers at Pfizer analyze lab results. The first dose of the Pfizer vaccine reduces the risk of transmitting COVID-19 by 75 percent.

they did. In addition, researchers don't yet know how long people may be immune to COVID-19 after receiving the vaccine. It's very likely that immunity lasts a short time, as does the influenza vaccine, and people will require yearly vaccinations. Dr. Adam Lauring, associate professor at the University of Michigan, said, "Even a short-term vaccine or something that prevents severe disease or protects only in the most vulnerable [people] would still be a game changer for this pandemic."

Coming up with a reliable vaccine is just one part of the puzzle. Distribution is the other part. The US alone has a population of more than 332 million, while the world population is more than 7 billion. Depending on the vaccine, either one or two doses is required. Manufacturers had to produce millions and millions of sterile glass vials and syringes. And it's vital that a vaccine reaches the global population as well. "We're not going to be safe as a world unless everywhere is safe," Dr. Seth Berkley, head of the international vaccine alliance GAVI, said. "So even if we had parts of the world that would have low spread or no spread, if you had large reservoirs of the virus in other places, of course you have a risk of reintroduction."

Confidence in the vaccines grew as they reached all parts of the US, carried on special flights by UPS and FedEx. Distribution of the vaccines began in the US on December 14, 2020. Hope blossomed across the country—hope that the end of the pandemic was in sight. However, hope dimmed slightly as the vaccine rollout fell far short of projections. The country seemed ill-prepared to vaccinate more than 332 million people. Staff and systems to do so were poorly coordinated. Websites to make appointments crashed in many states. Other locations reported elderly people waiting many hours, even overnight, in lines of cars extending several miles. In other cases, vaccination clinics were closed due to insufficient vaccine.

While the vaccine can last for up to six months if frozen, when thawed, it has a shelf life of about five days. State and federal mandates required that hospitals discard unused doses after those five days. Health-care workers tried to give as many doses as they could to patients, but often there were simply more vaccines about to expire than there were people who could receive them in time. Thousands, perhaps millions, of doses ended up in the trash. Even so, 13.4 percent of Americans had received their first vaccine, and 6 percent had received both doses, by February 23, 2021. Almost 80 percent of the vaccines that had been distributed to states had been administered. The remaining 20 percent was either in transit or cold storage waiting for administration.

WHO GETS THE VACCINE FIRST?

Jennifer Nuzzo, epidemiologist with Johns Hopkins Center for Health Security, said in October 2020, "It's not just the science of vaccine development we need to think about, but what it's going to take to get it to the people who need it." The CDC and other organizations such as the National Academy of Medicine developed plans to address that concern. The plans are similar in that they allocate the vaccines in phases. With other vaccines, there is usually no question about who will be vaccinated first or who last. For example, there's enough flu vaccine to go around for everyone who wants it. But supplies of the vaccine for SARS-CoV-2 will be limited—at least at the beginning— and tens of millions of Americans will need to be vaccinated.

The overall goal of the plan is to reduce severe illness and death, and to reduce the impact on society due to COVID-19. Ultimately, the decision was up to each state, although in general, phases were similar. Generally, these were the phases:

- Health-care workers, residents of long-term care facilities, and people over the age of seventy-five (or sixty-five in some states)
- First responders and people of all ages with underlying conditions that put them at significantly greater risk
- Teachers, school staff, and childcare workers; critical workers in essential high-risk settings; people of all ages with underlying conditions that put them at moderately high risk; people in homeless shelters, people with physical and mental health disabilities, people and staff in prisons; all older adults who did not yet receive the vaccine
- All other people over the age of sixteen who did not have access to vaccines in previous phases
- Children under the age of sixteen

HERD IMMUNITY

Vaccination is not the only way to become immune to a disease. Before vaccines for measles and chickenpox became common, people probably came down with those diseases when they were kids. The antibodies their bodies made to fight those diseases left them immune for decades, if not for the rest of their lives. These people, and people who received the measles vaccine, gave the US herd immunity. In herd immunity, a certain critical percentage of people are immune to a disease, making its spread from person to person uncommon. Then an entire community is protected, not just those who are immune.

Doctors know that getting COVID-19 might make a person immune to future infections. But unlike measles or chickenpox, doctors don't know how long immunity to COVID-19 lasts. A few people have had COVID-19 two times. Researchers say this likely happens more often than recognized. This is bad news for the herd immunity theory. If COVID-19 patients are immune from reinfection for only a few months, herd immunity would be short-lived. It means we must count on vaccination for herd immunity rather than people who have recovered from COVID-19. During a December 2020 interview, Fauci said, "If you really want true herd immunity, where you get a blanket of protection over the country . . . you want about 75 to 85 percent of the country to get vaccinated. I would say even closer to 85 percent."

New strains of the coronavirus threaten herd immunity. As SARS-CoV-2 circulates through the human population, it mutates and develops into slightly different variants. Variants emerged in the United Kingdom in late 2020. Others developed in South Africa and Brazil early in 2021. And at least seven newly identified variants are "home-grown" in the United States. Some variants are more contagious than the original strain, and others may turn

ON JANUARY 21, 2010, PRESIDENT BIDEN RELEASED A TWO-HUNDRED-PAGE NATIONAL PANDEMIC STRATEGY WITH GOALS THAT INCLUDED A COMPREHENSIVE VACCINATION CAMPAIGN, EXPANDED TESTING PROGRAMS, AND A MASK REQUIREMENT DURING INTERSTATE TRAVEL BY PLANES, TRAINS, FERRIES, AND PUBLIC TRANSPORTATION.

out to be more deadly. By early spring 2021, scientists had determined that the UK variant led to a 55 percent increase in deaths among those infected. Vaccines could still protect against the new strains, but it's unclear how effective they will be. Vaccine manufacturers considered the need to develop slightly altered vaccines to deal with the variants.

Vaccination of the majority of the population seems the only way to curb the COVID-19 pandemic. Experts warn that even with the vaccine, we should not relax measures to slow the spread of the virus, such as wearing masks, staying home whenever possible, maintaining social distancing, and washing hands. Vaccine distribution took months. Meanwhile, people continued to get infected in record numbers and to die. Taking steps to flatten the curve remained necessary even after the introduction of the vaccine.

FINDING A NEW NORMAL

After this horrendous COVID-19 pandemic, could life ever return to normal? Everyone's normal is different, but many normals include being able to go to school and see friends and talk to teachers in person. Normal means going to dances, sporting events, movies, and concerts. Normal means shopping for new clothes at a mall, going out to eat with friends, and hugging your family—without masks. People with jobs might define their normal as going back to work and chatting with coworkers about a project or holding meetings in person instead of over video. People who lost their jobs during the pandemic will look for ways to regain a steady income to try to return to their own normals.

A NEW SOCIETY?

Throughout 2020, schools, health-care providers, restaurants, retail stores, and offices learned how best to provide a safer environment

for the public and for their staff. Restaurants enhanced outdoor dining when indoor dining wasn't allowed. Many schools and offices introduced plastic partitions between desks and hand sanitizer in every room. Planes and medical offices may continue to use enhanced air purifiers. Often schools opened with a hybrid model in which students attended class in person for several hours a week, while attending virtually the rest of the time. Fewer students in classrooms allowed schools to space desks farther apart to provide social distancing. In spite of the disadvantages of not seeing friends or instructors, some students thrived with this hybrid model.

Home-based workers began selling expensive homes in big cities and moving to less costly homes in the suburbs or to smaller cities. One study showed as many as twenty-three million Americans planned to relocate because of the pandemic. Several large companies, including Facebook and Twitter, planned to allow their staff who worked at home during the pandemic to remain at home indefinitely. Mark Zuckerberg, head of Facebook, said half of its employees could be working remotely within the next five to ten years. Working at home during the pandemic showed it could be a good business model for some people. Twitter's Jennifer Christie said, "If our employees are in a role and situation that enables them to work from home and they want to continue to do so forever, we will make that happen. If not, our offices will be their warm and welcoming selves, with some additional precautions, when we feel it's safe to return."

Many smaller companies did the same. If people could work from home, companies could move to smaller offices, resulting in lower rent and utility bills. Some employees found they spent less on clothing to wear at home compared to what they would wear at the office. They spent less on gas because they didn't have to commute to work. And eating lunch at home cost less than a meal at a restaurant during a busy lunch hour. An NPR article said, "Tools such as Zoom

Most office workers shifted to working from home. Being isolated in the same space for a long time can have negative effects on people's mental health. But for many, the benefits included being able to spend more time with their families.

that have flourished during the pandemic create more flexibility in the workplace. White-collar jobs can be done anytime, anyplace, by any capable person with a phone and a laptop." Other people would prefer to work at their offices. Both options are likely to be offered as part of the new normal.

As employers terminated millions of full-time jobs at the start of the pandemic, many workers were forced into freelance work. While that may have suited some people, freelance workers often miss out on the benefits and health-care insurance that employers provide. Even so, 60 percent of freelancers said they want to stick to freelancing rather than return to a traditional job when the pandemic ends. Freelancers made up more than one-third of the workforce in 2020. The post-pandemic normal for the workplace may be a mix of people working at their place of employment, those

Thousands of businesses closed their doors permanently during the pandemic.

working at home for their employers, and freelancers who may do many kinds of work for many employers.

How about shopping? Clothing. Food. Household necessities. Would malls and grocery stores ever be the same after the pandemic? Many smaller stores and restaurants were forced out of business permanently during the pandemic. Those that struggled to stay open lost so much money their futures remained uncertain. In October 2020, Bill Ready, president of Google commerce, said, "Consumers have dramatically shifted their shopping to online over the past six months. Previously, many retailers might have said, 'E-commerce is a relatively small part of the overall business, maybe 10 percent.' That's grown dramatically to 30 percent or 40 percent plus for many retailers." Pandemic shopping included ordering clothing from online retailers and seeing it delivered a few days later. Grocery store shoppers asked for curbside pickup or home delivery. Many people preferred these ways of shopping. Will the big increase in online ordering and home delivery be the new normal for shopping?

PUBLIC HEALTH IN THE US

Public health is meant to protect the health of people. Agencies such as the CDC and the NIH are prime contributors to American health. Yet during the COVID-19 pandemic, politics interfered with their work as never before.

Past CDC directors soundly criticized the White House's handling of the pandemic. The lack of clear direction from Trump and his continued attacks on the CDC and other government organizations led to public mistrust of the CDC. Former CDC director Dr. William Foege said, "I think we've got about the worst response to this pandemic that you could possibly have." He stated the CDC's reputation had gone from gold to brass in just six months, and that it may be difficult for the agency to recruit top scientists for decades. "It's incredible that one person or a group of people can tarnish your reputation to that degree." The Trump administration also pressured CDC director Redfield to revise CDC guidelines on pandemic-related issues. And the administration blasted Fauci so often that he and his family received threats to their lives.

SURVIVING IN THE NEW NORMAL

People living through the pandemic realized that things were unlikely to be the same as before. Some things had changed forever. Fourteen-year-old Charlotte Bentley, who had to start her freshman year of high school with virtual learning, said her new normal is much different. "I'm definitely more aware of my health and of other people's health too. When I'm out in public I always wear my mask and if someone isn't wearing theirs, I notice. It's very hard not being able to hang out in groups, to go trick-or-treating, or to go to school. In a year I hope

[COVID-19] is over and I can return to school. I'll definitely be out and about more, and I'll be more aware of my surroundings."

Aidan Kirkman, also fourteen years old, said, "My new normal has been waking up, going straight to my computer, and 'going' to school. I can't even consider the idea of sleeping over at a friend's house or going outside without wearing a mask. I hope in a year I'll be able to see my friends, go to sporting events, and go to school in person."

Mia Harton only attended one week at Philadelphia's Temple University before it closed down. She had to return home for virtual classes. "My new normal right now is going to class online and completing my school work for most of the week. I haven't seen many of my friends. I hope to return to Temple in the spring semester [of 2021]. That would be my best new normal for the future."

Kris Obligar was still recovering from a severe case of COVID-19 months after she became infected. "My life has truly been flipped upside down. My new normal has been difficult to accept and I struggle with it every day. In a year I hope I'm able to simply do what I love: hiking, camping, backpacking, lifting weights. I love my family and friends and being able to hug them. Most of all, I love my health and I love breathing! I want to apply to graduate school to become a speech and language pathologist. Sharing my story is painful but I do so hoping to prevent anyone else from going through what I experienced. I hope people continue to take this disease seriously because it can affect everything in life."

Experts think the coronavirus may never go away, even after the vaccine—that it could circulate for decades among the world's population.

"THIS [PANDEMIC RESPONSE] HAS BEEN A MISMANAGED SITUATION EVERY STEP OF THE WAY. IT'S SHOCKING. IT'S UNBELIEVABLE—THE FACT THAT WE WOULD BE AMONG THE WORST IN THE WORLD."
—Bill Gates, 2020

WHAT WE'VE LEARNED FROM THE PANDEMIC

Few people knew what to expect when SARS-CoV-2 hit the world. But months later, the editor in chief of *Scientific American* summarized nine things we've learned.

- Outbreaks of COVID-19 can happen anywhere.
- COVID-19 can sicken and kill anyone.
- Contaminated surfaces are not the main danger.
- It is in the air.
- Many people are infectious without being sick.
- Warm summer weather will not stop the virus.
- Masks work.
- Racism, not race, is a risk factor.
- Misinformation kills.

Perhaps the virus will become less deadly as immunity spreads and our bodies adapt to it. But have we learned what we need to know to keep another pandemic from hitting humanity? Maureen Miller, epidemiologist with Columbia University, said, "Once this pandemic settles down, we're going to have a small window of opportunity to put in place infrastructure to prevent it from ever happening again."

Early in the pandemic, during the first major shutdowns and stay-at-home orders, people around the world noticed the air was cleaner. Greenhouse gas emissions fell, as did noise pollution. Wild animals sometimes roamed the streets of major cities. Distant mountains were once again visible. However, the pandemic also had a negative impact on the environment, especially with the increased use of plastics related to food delivery and pickup. Can the world learn a lesson and develop ways to use what we've learned in the pandemic to make lasting changes?

KRIS OBLIGAR'S RECOVERY

Kris Obligar, the twenty-seven-year-old speech therapy assistant who nearly died from COVID-19, is one of the lucky ones. Six months later, she celebrated her recovery and said:

Six months ago, I couldn't breathe and was put into an induced coma.

Five months ago, I woke up. I didn't have a voice and I was bed-ridden.

Four months ago, I couldn't get up from bed without being out of breath.

Three months ago, I couldn't walk more than a mile [1.6 km].

Two months ago, I couldn't climb a flight of stairs.

One month ago, I couldn't jog without having to stop to breathe.

Today I did something I used to love with the people I love. If you were to ask me three months ago, I would've told you that hiking and backpacking were a part of my past.

Today I proved myself wrong. Today I did more than I thought I was capable of.

To the year that taught me patience, grace, and understanding—you will not be missed.

Happy New Year everyone, please continue to do your due diligence. You've heard it before and I'll say it again. Please wear a mask, please trust science, please stay hydrated, & please don't be racist. 2021 will be looking a lot like 2020 if we can't get it together. Let's get it together. If I can, WE can.

Love, Kris

Tedros of the WHO hopes it's possible. In an August 2020 news conference, he said, "The COVID-19 pandemic has given new impetus to the need to accelerate efforts to respond to climate change. The COVID-19 pandemic has given us a glimpse of our world as it could be: cleaner skies and rivers." Wouldn't that be a wonderful way to turn all the bad news of the pandemic into some good news?

In January 2021, Kris Obligar celebrated her recovery from a severe case of COVID-19 by hiking at Lake Clementine, in Auburn, California.

GLOSSARY

antibodies: proteins in the bloodstream that the body produces to fight specific organisms, such as measles or COVID-19

bacteria: a large group of microscopic organisms that live in and on our body, and in the environment. Some are useful or harmless, and others cause serious diseases such as Lyme disease, strep throat, and sexually transmitted diseases.

Centers for Disease Control and Prevention (CDC): a branch of the US Department of Health and Human Services charged with investigating and controlling infectious disease in the nation

contact tracing: searching for people who were in contact with an infected person to help stop the disease from spreading

convalescent plasma: antibody-rich plasma (the liquid part of blood left after the removal of red blood cells) provided by COVID-19 survivors to help sick COVID-19 patients

coronavirus: a group of viruses with crownlike spikes. Some cause mild respiratory illnesses, while others cause serious and even deadly illnesses.

COVID-19: the illness caused by the SARS-CoV-2 virus, which triggered a pandemic in 2020

epidemiologist: a scientist who specializes in infectious diseases

essential workers: people working in health care, grocery stores, pharmacies, and other vital jobs such as emergency responders

flattening the curve: actions taken to slow down the spread of disease, such as wearing masks and social distancing

immunity: protection against a specific infectious organism either by vaccination or by having had the disease and developing antibodies against it

MERS-CoV: coronavirus that causes Middle East respiratory syndrome, a serious disease that kills more than a third of those it infects

National Institutes of Health (NIH): US health agency devoted to medical research; has twenty separate institutes including the National Institute of Allergy and Infectious Diseases

pandemic: an illness that affects people in many parts of the world at the same time

patient zero: the first known patient to have a disease. Epidemiologists try to find patient zero to help them identify the source of a disease.

positivity rate: the percentage of people tested for COVID-19 who were positive. Higher positivity rates indicate more widespread infection.

replication: formation of duplicate viruses as they invade host cells

SARS-CoV-1: a coronavirus that caused an epidemic with a 15 percent mortality rate in late 2002 and into 2003. It died out naturally.

SARS-CoV-2: a coronavirus that caused a pandemic that began in late 2019. It is less lethal than SARS-CoV-1 but far more contagious, infecting millions around the world.

social distancing: standing at least 6 feet (2 m) from people and avoiding large gatherings to help prevent the spread of an infectious disease

sputum: mucus that originates from the lower airways

T-cells: white blood cells that are part of immune systems to protect against infectious diseases

vaccination: the administration of a vaccine to provide immunity against a specific disease

vaccine: medication given to stimulate antibody production and provide immunity against a specific disease. Vaccines for viral diseases are less effective than vaccines for bacterial diseases.

virus: an infective microscopic organism that replicates only within another cell. It is much smaller and simpler than bacteria.

World Health Organization (WHO): an agency of the United Nations that is responsible for international public health

SOURCE NOTES

5 Ali S. Khan, *The Next Pandemic* (New York: PublicAffairs, 2016), 73.

5–6 Li Wenliang, quoted in Michael Bociurkiw, "China's Hero Doctor Was Punished for Telling Truth about Coronavirus," CNN, February 11, 2020, https://www.cnn .com/2020/02/08/opinions/coronavirus-bociurkiw/index.html.

6 Stephanie Hegarty, "The Chinese Doctor Who Tried to Warn Others about Coronavirus," BBC, February 6, 2020, https://www.bbc.com/news/world-asia -china-51364382.

6 Tom Inglesby, quoted in Andrew Green, "Li Wenliang Obituary," *Lancet* 395, no. 10225 (2020): 681, https://www.thelancet.com/journals/lancet/article /PIIS0140-6736(20)30382-2/fulltext/.

7 Linfa Wang, quoted in Michaeleen Doucleff, "WHO Points to Wildlife Farms in Southern China as Likely Source of Pandemic," NPR Goats and Soda, March 15, 2021, https://www.npr.org/sections/goatsandsoda/2021/03/15/977527808 /who-points-to-wildlife-farms-in-southwest-china-as-likely-source-of -pandemic/.

8 Jacqueline Alemany, "Power Up: President Trump and Secretary of State Mike Pompeo Continue to Push Unsubstantiated Wuhan Lab Theory on Novel Coronavirus Origins," *Washington Post*, May 4, 2020, https://www.washingtonpost.com/news /powerpost/paloma/powerup/2020/05/04/powerup-president-trump-and-secretary -of-state-mike-pompeo-continue-to-push-unsubstantiated-wuhan-lab-theory-on -novel-coronavirus-origins/5eaf5070602ff15fb00238b8/.

8 Mike Pompeo, *This Week*, ABC News, May 3, 2020, https://abcnews.go.com /Politics/week-transcript-20-mike-pompeo-gov-mike-dewine/story?id =70478442.

8 Geng Shuang, quoted in "Foreign Ministry Spokesperson Geng Shuang's Regular Press Conference," Ministry of Foreign Affairs of the People's Republic of China, April 28, 2020, https://www.fmprc.gov.cn/mfa_eng /xwfw_665399/s2510_665401/t1774380.shtml.

9 Jonna Mazet, quoted in Geoff Brumfiel and Emily Kwong, "Virus Researchers Cast Doubt on Theory of Coronavirus Lab Accident," NPR, April 23, 2020, https://www.npr.org/sections/goatsandsoda/2020/04/23/841729646/virus -researchers-cast-doubt-on-theory-of-coronavirus-lab-accident.

11   Larry Brilliant, quoted in "Unseen Enemy," CNN, 3:40, written and directed by Janet Tobias (New York: Sierra Tango Productions and Vulcan Productions, 2017).

17   David Quammen, "Did Pangolin Trafficking Cause the Coronavirus Pandemic?," *New Yorker*, August 24, 2020, https://www.newyorker.com /magazine/2020/08/31/did-pangolins-start-the-coronavirus-pandemic.

25   Marc Lipsitch, quoted in Jo Craven McGinty, "How Many People Might One Person with Coronavirus Infect?," *Wall Street Journal*, February 16, 2020, https://www.wsj.com/articles/how-many-people-might-one-person-with -coronavirus-infect-11581676200.

25   David Tyrrell and Steven Myint, in "Chapter 60, Coronaviruses," *Medical Microbiology*, 4th edition, ed. Samuel Baron (Galveston: University of Texas Medical Branch at Galveston, 1996), https://www.ncbi.nlm.nih.gov/books /NBK7782/.

28   Gro Harlem Brundtland, "World Health Organization Issues Emergency Travel Advisory," WHO news release, March 15, 2003, http://www.who.int /mediacentre/news/releases/2003/pr23/en/.

28–29   Sonia Shah, *Pandemic: Tracking Contagions, From Cholera to Ebola and Beyond* (New York: Farrar, Straus and Giroux, 2016), 51.

30   Erika Fry, "Contagion—How a Bat Virus Became a Human Killer," *Fortune*, August 22, 2014, http://fortune.com/2014/08/22/contagion-how-mers -became-a-human-killer/.

31   Ali Mohamed Zaki, quoted in Islam Hussein, "The Story of the First MERS Patient," Nature Middle East, June 2, 2014, https://www.natureasia.com/en /nmiddleeast/article/10.1038/nmiddleeast.2014.134.

35   Michael Osterholm, quoted in Carole Coleman, "Coronavirus Will Be with Us 'for All Eternity'—Expert," Ireland's National Public Service Media, August 16, 2020, https://www.rte.ie/news/2020/0816/1159506-coronavirus-experts -this-week/.

37   Adriana Heguy, quoted in Ryan W. Miller, "European Travelers Brought Coronavirus to New York Long Before First Case Confirmed, Studies Suggest," *USA Today*, April 9, 2020, https://www.usatoday.com/story/news/health /2020/04/09/new-york-coronavirus-cases-spread-months-came-europe -study/5120590002/.

37 Giuseppe Conte, quoted in Jason Horowitz, "How Italy Turned Around Its Coronavirus Calamity," *New York Times*, July 31, 2020, https://www.nytimes.com/2020/07/31/world/europe/italy-coronavirus-reopening.html.

42 Colleen Long, Gene Johnson, and Mike Corder, "Some US Producers, States Reopening amid Political Pressure," Associated Press, April 20, 2020, https://apnews.com/article/34b48ffba057099eaee794342bce448e/.

42 Bill Gates, "The First Modern Pandemic," *GatesNotes*, April 23, 2020, https://www.gatesnotes.com/Health/Pandemic-Innovation.

43 Erika Crisp, quoted in Michelle Marchante, "16 Friends Celebrated a Birthday at a Florida Bar. They Tested Positive for Coronavirus," *Miami Herald*, June 17, 2020, https://www.miamiherald.com/news/coronavirus/article243600032.html.

43 Tedros Adhanom Ghebreyesus, "WHO Director-General's Opening Remarks at the Media Briefing on COVID-19—27 July 2020," World Health Organization, accessed July 28, 2020, https://www.who.int/dg/speeches/detail/who-director-general-s-opening-remarks-at-the-media-briefing-on-covid-19---27-july-2020.

43 Helen Ouyang, "I'm an E.R. Doctor in New York. None of Us Will Ever Be the Same," *New York Times Magazine*, May 27, 2020, https://www.nytimes.com/2020/04/14/magazine/coronavirus-er-doctor-diary-new-york-city.html.

45 Anna Purna Kambhampaty, "'I Will Not Stand Silent.' 10 Asian Americans Reflect on Racism during the Pandemic and the Need for Equality," *Time*, June 25, 2020, https://time.com/5858649/racism-coronavirus/.

45 Kambhampaty.

46 "Health Equity Considerations and Racial and Ethnic Minority Groups," CDC, July 24, 2020, https://www.cdc.gov/coronavirus/2019-ncov/community/health-equity/race-ethnicity.html.

47 Michelle Tom, quoted in Christina Capatides, "Doctors Without Borders Dispatches Team to the Navajo Nation," CBS, May 11, 2020, https://www.cbsnews.com/news/doctors-without-borders-navajo-nation-coronavirus/.

47 Amy Segal, quoted in "MSF Hands Over Its COVID-19 Programs in the Navajo Nation and Pueblos," MSF, July 31, 2020, https://www.doctorswithoutborders.org/what-we-do/news-stories/news/msf-hands-over-its-covid-19-programs-navajo-nation-and-pueblos.

48   Terry Schultze, interview with the author, May 11, 2020.

48   Schultze.

48   Schultze.

48   Schultze.

49   Schultze.

51   Paul E. Peterson, quoted in "The Price Students Pay When Schools Are Closed," Harvard University Education Next, July 31, 2020, https://www.educationnext.org/price-students-pay-when-schools-are-closed/.

51–52   Charlotte Bentley, interview with the author, May 12, 2020.

52   Bentley.

52–53   Aidan Kirkman, interview with the author, May 19, 2020.

54   Amy Jacobsen, quoted in Joe Davidson, "Teacher Coaches Her Students to Get Help with Distance Learning," *Sacramento Bee*, September 17, 2020, https://www.pressreader.com/usa/the-sacramento-bee/20200917/textview.

54   Mia Harton, interview with the author, May 17, 2020.

54   Harton.

54–55   Harton, interview with the author, September 20, 2020.

55–56   JaNay Brown-Wood, interview with the author, September 20, 2020.

56   Lauren Hodges, "A Quiet and 'Unsettling' Pandemic Toll: Students Who've Fallen Off the Grid," NPR, December 29, 2020, https://www.npr.org/2020/12/29/948866982/a-quiet-and-unsettling-pandemic-toll-students-whove-fallen-off-the-grid.

56   Jack Kelly, quoted in "Mothers Share What Happens to Working Parents When the Schools Are Shut Down," *Forbes*, November 23, 2020, https://www.forbes.com/sites/jackkelly/2020/11/23/mothers-share-what-happens-to-working-parents-when-the-schools-are-shut-down/.

57–58   Benedict Carey, "For Some Teens, It's Been a Year of Anxiety and Trips to the E.R." *New York Times*, February 23, 2021, https://www.nytimes.com/2021/02/23/health/coronavirus-mental-health-teens.html.

59   Carey.

59   Davia Gray, "Teen Mental Health during Pandemic," Stanford Children's Health *Happier, Healthier Lives Blog*, December 11, 2020, https://healthier.stanfordchildrens.org/en/teen-mental-health-during-pandemic/.

59   Jennifer Heissenbuttel, quoted in Lulu Garcia-Navarro, "Missouri Teacher Who Died of COVID-19 Remembered by Her Sister," NPR, September 13, 2020, https://www.npr.org/2020/09/13/912424806/missouri-teacher-who-died-of -covid-19-remembered-by-her-sister.

61   Robert Redfield, quoted in Faith Karimi, Steve Almasy, and Dakin Andone, "Rushing Reopening Could Have Devastating Consequences, Dr. Fauci Says," CNN, August 13, 2020, https://www.cnn.com/2020/08/13/health/us -coronavirus-thursday/index.html.

61–62   "Dr. Anthony Fauci, at White House Briefing, March 10," C-SPAN, 7:02, March 10, 2020, https://www.c-span.org/video/?c4897554/user-clip-dr-tony-fauci -white-house-briefing-march-10.

63   Christopher Murray, quoted in Yasemin Saplakoglu, "Wear a Mask: You Could Help Save 66,000 Lives in the US," LiveScience.com, August 7, 2020, https:// www.livescience.com/wearing-masks-save-tens-thousands-lives.html.

64   National Geographic staff, "Poll: Who Always Wears a Mask in Public—and Who Doesn't?," *National Geographic*, July 10, 2020, https://www .nationalgeographic.com/science/2020/07/poll-covid-masks-morning -consult/.

64   Shawn Langlois, "'I Woke Up in a Free Country': Costco Shopper Gets Bounced from Store after Refusing to Wear a Mask," MarketWatch, May 23, 2020, https://www.marketwatch.com/story/i-woke-up-in-a-free-country -costco-shopper-gets-bounced-from-store-after-refusing-to-wear-a -mask-2020-05-19.

65   Robert Redfield, quoted in Miriam Berger et al., "Coronavirus Could Be 'Under Control' in Weeks If Everyone Wore Masks, CDC Director Says," *Washington Post*, July 14, 2020, https://www.washingtonpost.com/nation/2020/07/14 /coronavirus-live-updates-us/.

66   Henry Redel, quoted in John Brandon, "A Doctor Explains Why 45% of All Americans Refuse to Wear a Protective Mask," *Forbes*, May 6, 2020, https:// www.forbes.com/sites/johnbbrandon/2020/05/06/a-doctor-explains-why-45 -of-all-americans-refuse-to-wear-a-protective-mask/.

66   Kris Obligar, "I'll stick to a simple message for those that are still skeptical about COVID-19 . . . ," Facebook, posted July 29, 2020.

68   "Researchers Say Stay-at-Home Orders during Coronavirus Pandemic Have So Far Saved over 200,000 Lives," ASH Clinical News, June 12, 2020, https:// www.ashclinicalnews.org/online-exclusives/shutdown-orders-prevented -estimated-530-million-covid-19-infections-worldwide.

68 Solomon Hsiang, quoted in Edward Lempinen, "Emergency COVID-19 Measures Prevented More Than 500 Million Infections, Study Finds," Berkeley News, June 8, 2020, https://news.berkeley.edu/2020/06/08/emergency-covid-19-measures-prevented-more-than-500-million-infections-study-finds/.

69 Palli Thordarson, quoted in Brian Resnick, "How Soap Absolutely Annihilates the Coronavirus," Vox, March 27, 2020, https://www.vox.com/science-and-health/2020/3/11/21173187/coronavirus-covid-19-hand-washing-sanitizer-compared-soap-is-dope.

69 Colin Furness, quoted in Carolyn Crist, "Coronavirus Survives on Surfaces for Weeks: Study," WebMD, August 12, 2020, https://www.webmd.com/lung/news/20201012/coronavirus-survives-on-surfaces-for-weeks-study.

71 Office of Governor Gavin Newsom, "Governor Newsom Announces Major Plan to More Than Double State's Testing Capacity, Reduce Turnaround Time," press release, August 26, 2020, https://www.gov.ca.gov/2020/08/26/governor-newsom-announces-major-plan-to-more-than-double-states-testing-capacity-reduce-turnaround-time/.

72 Amy Driscoll, quoted in Holly Yan, "Contact Tracing 101: How It Works, Who Could Get Hired, and Why It's So Critical in Fighting Coronavirus Now," CNN, May 15, 2020, https://www.cnn.com/2020/04/27/health/contact-tracing-explainer-coronavirus/index.html.

73 Amit Kaushal and Russ B. Altman, "Can Contact Tracing Work at COVID Scale?," *Health Affairs Blog*, July 8, 2020, https://www.healthaffairs.org/do/10.1377/hblog20200630.746159/full/.

75 Thomas Smith, "A Supercomputer Analyzed Covid-19—and an Interesting New Theory Has Emerged," Elemental, August 31, 2020, https://elemental.medium.com/a-supercomputer-analyzed-covid-19-and-an-interesting-new-theory-has-emerged-31cb8eba9d63.

76 Jose Pascual, quoted in Ariana Eunjung Cha, "Doctors Express Glimmers of Hope as They Try Out New Approaches against Coronavirus," *Washington Post*, May 13, 2020, https://www.washingtonpost.com/health/2020/05/13/coronavirus-treatments/.

77–78 Branko Zlatar, quoted in Sawsan Morrar and Tony Bizjak, "She's Only 27—and COVID-19 Nearly Killed Her. She Wants Her Story to Be a Lesson," *Sacramento Bee*, July 30, 2020, https://www.sacbee.com/news/coronavirus/article244533562.html.

80 Alyssa Milano (@milano_alyssa), "This was me on April 2nd after being sick for 2 weeks . . . ," Instagram, August 5, 2020, https://www.instagram.com/p/CDhQ43NgPO2/.

82 Alan Kliger, quoted in Lenny Bernstein et al., "Coronavirus Destroys Lungs. But Doctors Are Finding Its Damage in Kidneys, Hearts and Elsewhere," *Washington Post*, April 15, 2020, https://www.washingtonpost.com/health/coronavirus-destroys-lungs-but-doctors-are-finding-its-damage-in-kidneys-hearts-and-elsewhere/2020/04/14/7ff71ee0-7db1-11ea-a3ee-13e1ae0a3571_story.html.

82–83 Valentina Puntmann, quoted in Elizabeth Cooney, "Covid-19 Infections Leave an Impact on the Heart, Raising Concerns about Lasting Damage," Stat, July 27, 2020, https://www.statnews.com/2020/07/27/covid19-concerns-about-lasting-heart-damage/.

83 Stephen Nesbitt, quoted in Nelson Oliveira, "Indiana College Student, 20, Found Dead in Dorm Room Had Coronavirus, Never Got Test Results," *New York Daily News*, November 4, 2020, https://www.nydailynews.com/news/national/ny-indiana-college-student-found-dead-in-dorm-room-had-coronavirus-20201104-n3ajcus5szb7rmaa2dkuz3bcju-story.html.

83–84 Angela Rasmussen, quoted in Lenny Bernstein and Ariana Eunjung Cha, "Doctors Keep Discovering New Ways the Coronavirus Attacks the Body," *Washington Post*, May 10, 2020, https://www.washingtonpost.com/health/2020/05/10/coronavirus-attacks-body-symptoms/.

84 Adapted from Sanjay Gupta, CNN chief medical correspondent, "5 Common Coronavirus Misconceptions and the Science You Need to Know," CNN, September 26, 2020, https://www.cnn.com/2020/09/26/health/coronavirus-myths-science-gupta/index.html.

88 Stephen M. Hahn, "FDA Approves First Treatment for COVID-19," FDA, news release, October 22, 2020, https://www.fda.gov/news-events/press-announcements/fda-approves-first-treatment-covid-19.

88 Chauncey Crandall, *Beat the Coronavirus: Fight Back* (West Palm Beach, FL: Humanix Books, 2020), 96–97.

88 Crandall, 94–95.

90 Simone Hannah-Clark, "An I.C.U. Nurse's Coronavirus Diary," *New York Times*, April 3, 2020, https://www.nytimes.com/2020/04/03/opinion/sunday/coronavirus-icu-nurse.html?.

91 Noah Weiland and Maggie Haberman, "Oracle Providing White House with Software to Study Unproven Coronavirus Drugs," *Washington Post*, March 24, 2020, https://www.nytimes.com/2020/03/24/us/politics/trump-oracle -coronavirus-chloroquine.html.

91 Weiland and Haberman.

92 Mohammad Sultan Khuroo, "Chloroquine and Hydroxychloroquine in Coronavirus Disease 2019 (COVID-19)," *International Journal of Antimicrobial Agents* 56, no. 3 (September 2020): 106101, https://www.ncbi.nlm.nih.gov /pmc/articles/PMC7366996/.

92 Weiland and Haberman, "Oracle."

92 Donald Trump, quoted in Dartunorro Clark, "Trump Suggests 'Injection' of Disinfectant to Beat Coronavirus and 'Clean' the Lungs," NBC, April 24, 2020, https://www.nbcnews.com/politics/donald-trump/trump-suggests-injection -disinfectant-beat-coronavirus-clean-lungs-n1191216.

92 Robert Glatter, quoted in "Calls to Poison Centers Spike after the President's Comments about Using Disinfectants to Treat Coronavirus," *Forbes*, April 25, 2020, https://www.forbes.com/sites/robertglatter/2020/04/25/calls-to-poison -centers-spike--after-the-presidents-comments-about-using-disinfectants -to-treat-coronavirus/.

93 Donald Trump, quoted in Brett Samuels, "Trump Suggests Using Light, Heat as Coronavirus Treatment," MSN, April 23, 2020, https://www.msn.com/en-in /news/world/trump-suggests-using-light-heat-as-coronavirus-treatment /ar-BB137q6N.

94 Cassandra Quave, quoted in Aristos Georgiou, "Don't Take 'Dangerous' Oleandrin for COVID-19 Experts Warn, after Trump Says 'We'll Look at It,'" *Newsweek*, August 20, 2020, https://www.newsweek.com/dont-take -dangerous-oleandrin-covid-19-experts-warn-1526453.

94–95 Tom Frieden et al., "We Ran the CDC. No President Ever Politicized Its Science the Way Trump Has," *Washington Post*, July 14, 2020, https://www .washingtonpost.com/outlook/2020/07/14/cdc-directors-trump-politics/.

95 Frieden et al.

97 Peter Piot, quoted in Dirk Draulans, "'Finally a Virus Got Me,' Scientist Who Fought Ebola and HIV Reflects on Facing Death from COVID-19," *Science*, May 8, 2020, https://www.sciencemag.org/news/2020/05/finally-virus-got-me -scientist-who-fought-ebola-and-hiv-reflects-facing-death-covid-19.

98   German Lopez, "Your State's Covid-19 Epidemic, Explained in 4 Maps," Vox, December 9, 2020, https://www.vox.com/future-perfect/2020/7/31/21340268/coronavirus-pandemic-covid-state-maps-charts-data.

100   Catie Carrigan, quoted in Sarah Fowler, "What Seven ICU Nurses Want You to Know about the Battle against COVID-19," *Washington Post*, December 7, 2020, https://www.washingtonpost.com/graphics/2020/national/icu-nurses-covid-19/.

102   Lauran Neergaard, "Years of Research Laid Groundwork for Speedy COVID-19 Vaccines," PBS, December 7, 2020, https://www.pbs.org/newshour/health/years-of-research-laid-groundwork-for-speedy-covid-19-vaccines.

103   Monika Evstatieva, "Anatomy of a COVID-19 Conspiracy Theory," NPR, July 10, 2020, https://www.npr.org/2020/07/10/889037310/anatomy-of-a-covid-19-conspiracy-theory.

103   Evstatieva.

103   Sy Mukherjee, "Where the 4 Major Coronavirus Vaccine Candidates Currently Stand," Fortune, September 23, 2020, https://fortune.com/2020/09/23/coronavirus-vaccine-candidates-pfizer-biontech-moderna-j-and-j-astrazeneca-oxford/.

104   Kelly Moore, quoted in John Bonifield, Elizabeth Cohen, and Dana Vigue, "One Shot of Coronavirus Vaccine Likely Won't Be Enough," CNN, August 30, 2020, https://www.cnn.com/2020/08/30/health/coronavirus-vaccine-two-doses/index.html.

104   Sandra Lindsay, quoted in Sharon Otterman, "'I Trust Science,' Says Nurse Who Is First to Get Vaccine in US," *New York Times*, December 14, 2020, https://www.nytimes.com/2020/12/14/nyregion/us-covid-vaccine-first-sandra-lindsay.html.

105   Adam Lauring, quoted in Kelly Malcom, "Should We Worry about COVID-19 Reinfection?," University of Michigan Health, September 11, 2020, https://labblog.uofmhealth.org/rounds/should-we-worry-about-covid-19-reinfection.

105–106 Seth Berkley, quoted in Joe Palca, "When Can We Expect a Coronavirus Vaccine?," NPR, May 12, 2020, https://knpr.org/npr/2020-05/when-can-we-expect-coronavirus-vaccine.

106   Jennifer Nuzzo, quoted in Sarah Elizabeth Richards, "Who Will Get the Vaccine First? Here's Where You Might Land in Line," *National Geographic*, October 14, 2020, https://www.nationalgeographic.com/science/2020/10/who-is-first-in-line-coronavirus-vaccine/.

108   Anthony Fauci, quoted in Dylan Scott, "Fauci: 85 Percent of the US Needs to Get the COVID-19 Vaccine for 'True Herd Immunity,'" Vox, December 15, 2020, https://www.vox.com/coronavirus-covid19/2020/12/15/22176555/anthony -fauci-covid-19-vaccine-herd-immunity-goal.

111   Martin Blaser, "What Will the Coronavirus 'New Normal' Look Like?," Rutgers University news release, July 15, 2020, https://www.rutgers.edu/news/how -live-our-new-normal-covid-19.

112   Jennifer Christie, quoted in Rob McLean, "These Companies Plan to Make Working from Home the New Normal," CNN, July 25, 2020, https://www.cnn .com/2020/05/22/tech/work-from-home-companies/index.html.

112–113   Uri Berliner, "Jobs in the Pandemic: More Are Freelance and May Stay That Way Forever," NPR, September 16, 2020, https://www.npr.org/2020/09/16 /912744566/jobs-in-the-pandemic-more-are-freelance-and-may-stay-that -way-forever.

114   Bill Ready, quoted in Charles Riley, "Online Shopping Has Been Turbocharged by the Pandemic. There's No Going Back," CNN, October 13, 2020, https:// www.cnn.com/2020/10/11/investing/stocks-week-ahead/index.html.

115   William Foege, quoted in Pien Huang, "Past CDC Director Urges Current One to Stand Up to Trump," NPR, October 8, 2020, https://www.npr.org/sections /coronavirus-live-updates/2020/10/08/921872526/past-cdc-director-urges -current-one-to-stand-up-to-trump.

115–116   Charlotte Bentley, interview with the author, November 1, 2020.

116   Aidan Kirkman, interview with the author, October 28, 2020.

116   Mia Harton, interview with the author, October 26, 2020.

116   Kris Obligar, interview with the author, October 28, 2020.

116   Bill Gates, quoted in Helen Branswell, "Bill Gates Slams 'Shocking' US Response to Covid-19 Pandemic," Stat, September 14, 2020, https://www .statnews.com/2020/09/14/bill-gates-slams-mismanaged-u-s-response-to -covid-19-pandemic/.

117   Laura Helmuth, "Nine Important Things We've Learned about the Coronavirus Pandemic So Far," Scientific American, September 5, 2020, https://www .scientificamerican.com/article/nine-important-things-weve-learned-about -the-coronavirus-pandemic-so-far/.

117   Maureen Miller, quoted in Charlie Campbell, Yuxi Yunnan, and Alice Park, "Inside the Global Quest to Trace the Origins of COVID-19—and Predict Where It Will Go Next," Time, July 23, 2020, https://time.com/5870481/coronavirus-origins/.

118 Kris Obligar, "Six months ago, I couldn't breathe and was put into an induced coma . . . ," Facebook, posted January 1, 2021.

119 Tedros Adhanom Ghebreyesus, quoted in Berkeley Lovelace Jr., "WHO Warns Coronavirus Vaccine Alone Won't End Pandemic: 'We Cannot Go Back to the Way Things Were.'" CNBC, August 21, 2020, https://www.cnbc.com/2020/08/21 /who-warns-a-coronavirus-vaccine-alone-will-not-end-pandemic.html.

SELECTED BIBLIOGRAPHY

Alemany, Jacqueline. "Power Up: President Trump and Secretary of State Mike Pompeo Continue to Push Unsubstantiated Wuhan Lab Theory on Novel Coronavirus Origins." *Washington Post*, May 4, 2020. https://www.washingtonpost.com/news/powerpost /paloma/powerup/2020/05/04/powerup-president-trump-and-secretary-of-state-mike -pompeo-continue-to-push-unsubstantiated-wuhan-lab-theory-on-novel-coronavirus -origins/5eaf5070602ff15fb00238b8/.

Beaubien, Jason. "Why They're Called 'Wet Markets'—and What Health Risks They Might Pose." NPR, January 31, 2020. https://www.npr.org/sections/goatsandsoda /2020/01/31/800975655/why-theyre-called-wet-markets-and-what-health-risks-they -might-pose.

Bernstein, Lenny, and Ariana Eunjung Cha. "Doctors Keep Discovering New Ways the Coronavirus Attacks the Body." *Washington Post*, May 10, 2020. https://www .washingtonpost.com/health/2020/05/10/coronavirus-attacks-body-symptoms/.

Bernstein, Lenny, Carolyn Y. Johnson, Sarah Kaplan, and Laurie McGinley. "Coronavirus Destroys Lungs. But Doctors Are Finding Its Damage in Kidneys, Hearts and Elsewhere." *Washington Post*, April 15, 2020. https://www.washingtonpost.com/health /coronavirus-destroys-lungs-but-doctors-are-finding-its-damage-in-kidneys-hearts -and-elsewhere/2020/04/14/7ff71ee0-7db1-11ea-a3ee-13e1ae0a3571_story.html.

Blaser, Martin. "What Will the Coronavirus 'New Normal' Look Like?" Rutgers University, news release, July 15, 2020. https://www.rutgers.edu/news/how-live-our-new-norma l-covid-19.

Bociurkiw, Michael. "China's Hero Doctor Was Punished for Telling Truth about Coronavirus." CNN, February 11, 2020. https://www.cnn.com/2020/02/08/opinions /coronavirus-bociurkiw/index.html.

Bonifield, John, Elizabeth Cohen, and Dana Vigue. "One Shot of Coronavirus Vaccine Likely Won't Be Enough." CNN, August 30, 2020. https://www.cnn.com/2020/08/30/health/coronavirus-vaccine-two-doses/index.html.

Brandon, John. "A Doctor Explains Why 45% of all Americans Refuse to Wear a Protective Mask." *Forbes*, May 6, 2020. https://www.nationalgeographic.com/science/2020/07/poll-covid-masks-morning-consult/.

Branswell, Helen. "Bill Gates Slams 'Shocking' U.S. Response to Covid-19 Pandemic." Stat, September 14, 2020. https://www.statnews.com/2020/09/14/bill-gates-slams-mismanaged-u-s-response-to-covid-19-pandemic/.

Brilliant, Larry. "Unseen Enemy." CNN documentary video, 3:40. New York: Sierra Tango Productions and Vulcan Productions, 2017.

Brumfiel, Geoff, and Emily Kwong. "Virus Researchers Cast Doubt on Theory of Coronavirus Lab Accident." NPR, April 23, 2020. https://www.npr.org/sections/goatsandsoda/2020/04/23/841729646/virus-researchers-cast-doubt-on-theory-of-coronavirus-lab-accident.

Capatides, Christina. "Doctors Without Borders Dispatches Team to the Navajo Nation." CBS, May 11, 2020. https://www.cbsnews.com/news/doctors-without-borders-navajo-nation-coronavirus/.

Cha, Ariana Eunjung. "Superspreading' Events, Triggered by People Who May Not Even Know They Are Infected, Propel Coronavirus Pandemic." *Washington Post*, July 18, 2020. https://www.washingtonpost.com/health/2020/07/18/coronavirus-superspreading-events-drive-pandemic/.

Coleman, Carole. "Coronavirus Will Be with Us 'for All Eternity'—Expert." Ireland's National Public Service Media, August 16, 2020. https://www.rte.ie/news/2020/0816/1159506-coronavirus-experts-this-week/.

Coronavirus Resource Center. Johns Hopkins. Accessed March 25, 2021. https://coronavirus.jhu.edu/.

Crandall, Chauncy. *Beat the Coronavirus: Fight Back*. West Palm Beach, FL: Humanix Books, 2020.

Frieden, Tom, Jeffrey Koplan, David Satcher, and Richard Besser. "We Ran the CDC. No President Ever Politicized Its Science the Way Trump Has." *Washington Post*, July 14, 2020. https://www.washingtonpost.com/outlook/2020/07/14/cdc-directors-trump-politics/.

Fry, Erika. "Contagion—How a Bat Virus Became a Human Killer." *Fortune,* August 22, 2014. http://fortune.com/2014/08/22/contagion-how-mers-became-a-human-killer/.

Guarino, Ben. "Six Feet May Not Be Enough to Protect against Coronavirus, Experts Warn." *Washington Post*, August 27, 2020.

Huang, Pien. "Why the Novel Coronavirus Has the Power to Launch a Pandemic." NPR, July 29, 2020. https://www.npr.org/sections/goatsandsoda/2020/07/29/888957450/why-the-novel-coronavirus-has-the-power-to-launch-a-pandemic.

Hussein, Islam. "The Story of the First MERS Patient." Nature Middle East, June 2, 2014. https://www.natureasia.com/en/nmiddleeast/article/10.1038/nmiddleeast.2014.134.

"Influenza: Are We Ready?" WHO. Accessed March 25, 2021. https://www.who.int/news-room/spotlight/influenza-are-we-ready;

"Influenza (Seasonal)." WHO, November 6, 2018. https://www.who.int/en/news-room/fact-sheets/detail/influenza-(seasonal).

Kambhampaty, Anna Purna. "'I Will Not Stand Silent.' 10 Asian Americans Reflect on Racism during the Pandemic and the Need for Equality." *Time*, June 25, 2020. https://time.com/5858649/racism-coronavirus/.

Khan, Ali S. *The Next Pandemic.* New York: PublicAffairs, 2016.

Lovelace, Berkeley, Jr. "WHO Warns Coronavirus Vaccine Alone Won't End Pandemic." *CNBC,* August 21, 2020. https://www.cnbc.com/2020/08/21/who-warns-a-coronavirus-vaccine-alone-will-not-end-pandemic.html.

Mandaville, Apoorva. "Why Does the Coronavirus Hit Men Harder? A New Clue." *New York Times*, August 26, 2020. https://www.nytimes.com/2020/08/26/health/coronavirus-men-immune.html.

McLean, Rob. "These Companies Plan to Make Working from Home the New Normal." *CNN,* June 25, 2020. https://www.cnn.com/2020/05/22/tech/work-from-home-companies/index.html.

"Middle East Respiratory Syndrome Coronavirus (MERS-CoV)." WHO. Accessed March 25, 2021. https://www.who.int/emergencies/mers-cov/en/.

Miller, Ryan W. "European Travelers Brought Coronavirus to New York Long Before First Case Confirmed, Studies Suggest." *USA Today*, April 9, 2020. https://www.usatoday.com/story/news/health/2020/04/09/new-york-coronavirus-cases-spread-months-came-europe-study/5120590002/.

Milling, Marla. "Researchers Say Stay-at-Home Orders during Coronavirus Pandemic Have So Far Saved over 200,000 Lives." *Forbes*, May 19, 2020. https://www.forbes.com /sites/marlamilling/2020/05/19/stay-at-home-orders-saves-hundreds-of-thousands-of -lives-report-confirms/.

National Geographic staff. "Poll: Who Always Wears a Mask in Public—and Who Doesn't?" *National Geographic*, July 10, 2020. https://www.nationalgeographic.com /science/2020/07/poll-covid-masks-morning-consult/.

Popkin, Barry M., Shufa Du, William D. Green, Melinda A. Beck, Taghred Algaith, Christopher H. Herbst, Reem F. Alsukait et al. "Individuals with Obesity and COVID-19: A Global Perspective on the Epidemiology and Biological Relationships." *Obesity Reviews,* August 26, 2020. https://onlinelibrary.wiley.com/doi/full/10.1111/obr.13128.

Quammen, David. "Why Weren't We Ready for the Coronavirus?" *New Yorker*. May 4, 2020. https://www.newyorker.com/magazine/2020/05/11/why-werent-we-ready-for -the-coronavirus.

Richards, Sarah Elizabeth. "Who Will Get the Vaccine First? Here's Where You Might Land in Line." *National Geographic*, October 14, 2020. https://www.nationalgeographic.com /science/2020/10/who-is-first-in-line-coronavirus-vaccine/.

Riley, Charles. "Online Shopping Has Been Turbocharged by the Pandemic." CNN, October 13, 2020. https://www.cnn.com/2020/10/11/investing/stocks-week-ahead/index.html.

"SARS Basics Fact Sheet." CDC, December 6, 2017. https://www.cdc.gov/sars/about /fs-sars.html.

Segal, Amy, "MSF Hands Over Its COVID-19 Programs in the Navajo Nation and Pueblos." MSF, July 31, 2020. https://www.doctorswithoutborders.org/what-we-do/news-stories /news/msf-hands-over-its-covid-19-programs-navajo-nation-and-pueblos.

Shah, Sonia. *Pandemic: Tracking Contagions, from Cholera to Ebola and Beyond*. New York: Farrar, Straus and Giroux, 2016.

Tedros Adhanom Ghebreyesus. "WHO Director-General's Opening Remarks at the Media Briefing on COVID-19—27 July 2020." World Health Organization, July 27, 2020. https:// www.who.int/dg/speeches/detail/who-director-general-s-opening-remarks-at-the -media-briefing-on-covid-19---27-july-2020.

Yan, Holly. "Contact Tracing 101: How It Works, Who Could Get Hired, and Why It's So Critical in Fighting Coronavirus Now." CNN, May 15, 2020. https://www.cnn.com /2020/04/27/health/contact-tracing-explainer-coronavirus/index.html.

FURTHER INFORMATION

BOOKS

Craig, Erin A. *Together, Apart*. New York: Delacorte, 2020.
This YA anthology of fiction contains stories set during the pandemic. The book features nine romantic stories with the characters navigating their new normal: social distancing, virtual classrooms, baking, walking, and missing out on the prom. While the seriousness of the pandemic is presented, so is hope for a future with a new partner.

Dinmont, Kerry. *Frontline Workers during Covid-19*. San Diego: Brightpoint, 2021.
While many people began working from home during the COVID-19 pandemic, others had no choice but to remain at the jobsite. These included health-care workers, first responders (EMTs, firefighters, and police) as well as grocery store clerks and delivery drivers. Learn what the pandemic was like for these frontline workers.

Goldsmith, Connie. *Pandemic: How Climate, the Environment, and Superbugs Increase the Risk.* Minneapolis: Twenty-First Century Books, 2019.
Throughout history, several deadly pandemics brought humanity to its knees, killing millions. Read about factors that contribute to the spread of disease such as climate change, disruption of animal habitats, and increased travel.

Lasica, Joseph D. *Beat the Coronavirus: Strategies for Staying Safe and Coping with the New Normal during the COVID-19 Pandemic*. New York: Socialbrite, 2020.
This handbook for learning to live with the pandemic answers dozens of questions readers might have such as What's the best way to protect myself from COVID-19? How do I protect my grandparents from catching it? and What are the signs that I might have the virus?

MacKenzie, Debora. *COVID-19: The Pandemic That Never Should Have Happened and How to Stop the Next One.* New York: Hachette Books, 2020.
Debora MacKenzie, a scientist journalist, reports on how we had ample time to prepare for the coronavirus outbreak, but failed to heed the lessons of the past. The results is the COVID-19 pandemic. Read how COVID-19 moved from a manageable outbreak to a global pandemic in just weeks.

Marcovitz, Hal. *The Covid-19 Pandemic: The World Turned Upside Down.* San Diego: Referencepoint, 2020.

The new virus infected millions within weeks of its appearance late in 2019. Through personal accounts and expert interviews, Marcovitz reviews the origin of the pandemic and how it turned the world upside down. Read about deserted highways, empty schools and offices, and canceled sporting events.

Ray, Sammy. *2020 Pandemic Quarantine Sketchbook with Drawing Prompts for Artists.* Independently published, 2020.

The book features fifty prompts to inspire artists with pages that work for pens, pencils, crayons, colored pencils, and watercolor. Teens and adults can sketch, draw, paint, doodle, or write about their experiences during the pandemic.

WEBSITES AND ORGANIZATIONS

Center for Health Journalism

https://centerforhealthjournalism.org/blog-category/coronavirus-files
The site provides analysis on the pandemic. It offers dozens of articles written by top journalists who specialize in health and science writing. Articles of special interest include information about young adults in the pandemic, how COVID-19 affects people of color, and outbreaks on college campuses.

Center for Infectious Disease Research and Policy (CIDRAP)

https://www.cidrap.umn.edu/covid-19/podcasts-webinars
CIDRAP's mission is to prevent illness and death from targeted infectious disease threats by offering scientific information in an accessible format. One of the nation's most influential infectious experts, Michael Osterholm, presents a series of podcasts about COVID-19. Lasting about an hour each, listeners can select from dozens of episodes focusing on the virus and its effects.

Centers for Disease Control and Prevention (CDC)

https://www.cdc.gov/coronavirus/2019-ncov/index.html
The CDC's coronavirus website offers a wealth of information about the virus, the pandemic, your health, and the health of teens and young adults. It also provides checklists for going back to school, symptoms to watch out for, how to care for others with COVID-19, and statistical data. The site describes testing for COVID-19 and vaccine development.

Johns Hopkins University & Medicine

https://coronavirus.jhu.edu/

This prestigious university tracks COVID-19 cases for every state. This information is ideal for someone needing more detail about a particular state or region. It also offers sections on contact tracing, vaccine development, flattening the curve, and the early days of the pandemic in China. The site provides many interesting maps and graphs showing the status of the pandemic at different times.

Mayo Clinic

https://www.mayoclinic.org/coronavirus-covid-19

Learn how to tell the difference between COVID-19 and flu, and when to see a doctor. See the risk factors associated with severe illness, review ideas about prevention, common symptoms, and how to get emergency care if needed. The site describes the most common treatments for the coronavirus and the clinical trials that Mayo Clinic participates in. A map shows the case rate and positivity rate for the United States.

National Institute of Allergy and Infectious Disease

https://www.niaid.nih.gov/diseases-conditions/coronaviruses

Dr. Anthony Fauci, one of the most influential infectious disease experts in the nation, heads up this institute, which is part of the National Institutes of Health. The site has numerous articles about the pandemic and talks about clinical trials that can help develop better treatments for COVID-19.

Nemours Teen Health

https://teenshealth.org/en/teens/coronavirus-calm.html

This organization has a concise page of valuable information about the pandemic, describing social distancing, wearing a mask, staying in touch with people, and other things a teen can do. The same page offers links to sections about stress and anxiety to help teens cope with the realities of the pandemic.

World Health Organization (WHO)

https://www.who.int/emergencies/diseases/novel-coronavirus-2019

This excellent site provides advice for the public such as how to travel safely and discusses the pros and cons of holding gatherings. It dispels dozens of myths about COVID-19, such as that hot peppers and garlic can cure the disease, and that houseflies can carry the virus.

https://www.who.int/vaccine_safety/initiative/detection/immunization
_misconceptions/en/

This WHO educational website reviews the six common misconceptions people may have about the COVID-19 vaccines. It offers factual information to ease fears of those concerned about the effects of vaccinations.

Worldometer

https://www.worldometers.info/coronavirus/

This site is filled with information about the pandemic around the world, including case counts, deaths, and recovery in every country. Graphs and maps allow the user to see the entire world or only one country and are updated daily. You can choose to view the information in different formats. It also provides a table showing how age affects the number of cases and their outcome by gender (61.8 percent of deaths are male, and 38.2 percent are female).

AUDIO, MOVIES, AND VIDEOS

"Alyssa Milano's Long Haul COVID-19 Battle." YouTube video, 4:04. Posted by 60 MinutesAustralia, September 22, 2020. https://www.youtube.com/watch?v=PAxufz3476o.

Actor Alyssa Milano talks about her monthslong battle with COVID-19. She estimates she's lost 40 percent of her health since she came down with the disease and wonders if she'll ever fully recover.

"Can Dogs Detect the Novel Coronavirus?" *Washington Post*, August 18, 2020. 2:49. https://www.washingtonpost.com/science/2020/08/18/dogs-sniff-coronavirus-detection/.

Watch how a dog learns to sniff out the coronavirus with 95 percent accuracy in a University of Pennsylvania lab. Airports may use trained dogs to detect coronavirus in air travelers.

Coronavirus in Navajo Nation. CBS News, May 11, 2020. 27:05. https://www.cbsnews.com/news/doctors-without-borders-navajo-nation-coronavirus/.

See what life is like in the rural Navajo Nation. The nation asked the US government for help early in the pandemic but received no answer. The international aid organization Doctors Without Borders responded—the first time the organization has helped people in the US.

"Dr. Anthony Fauci, at White House Briefing, March 10." C-SPAN, March 10, 2020. https://www.c-span.org/video/?c4897554/user-clip-dr-tony-fauci-white-house-briefing-march-10.

Dr. Anthony Fauci of the NIH talks about community spread in Florida. Viewers can select either video or read transcripts of the briefing.

"How the Novel Coronavirus Hijacks Our Defenses." NPR, May 5, 2020. 5:10. https://
www.npr.org/sections/health-shots/2020/05/05/850361325/video-how-the-novel
-coronavirus-hijacks-our-defenses/.
The video shows how lungs work and describes viruses in general, as well as the
novel coronavirus that causes COVID-19. Viruses persist by commandeering human
cells and forcing them to produce new virus particles.

"An Introduction to COVID-19 Tests." US Food and Drug Administration. Accessed
December 9, 2020. 2:48. https://www.fda.gov/consumers/consumer-updates
/coronavirus-testing-basics.
This short video explains the difference between diagnostic and antibody testing.
The first shows if a person currently has COVID-19, while the second shows if a
person has had COVID-19 in the past.

"It's Okay to Be Smart. How Well Do Masks Work? *(Schlieren Imaging in Slow Motion!)*."
YouTube video, 8:20. Posted by It's Okay to Be Smart, July 4, 2020. https://www
.youtube.com/watch?v=0Tp0zB904Mc.
Watch experiments with different types of masks to see how they control—or don't
control—the spread of the coronavirus in aerosol droplets.

"My Family amidst the COVID-19 Pandemic—Mia." YouTube video, 5:13. Posted by
Megan Harton, April 2020. https://www.youtube.com/watch?v=sFjSCpizRgQ.
Watch how seventeen-year-old Mia Harton coped with the early shutdown of the
country in April 2020. Filmed in Vermont, the video depicts the empty streets,
parks, and malls so common at that time. Mia talks about the things she and her
family did to help with the isolation.

"Tell Me More about Vaccines." US Department of Health and Human Services. Accessed
December 9, 2020. 6.32. https://www.youtube.com/embed/Z06JQhyZLUI?rel=0.
Narrated by Dr. Anthony Fauci, the video describes the development and clinical
testing of potential vaccines for SARS-CoV-2.

"Why Aerosol vs. Droplet Transmission of Coronavirus Matters." *Washington Post*,
September 21, 2020. 2:56. https://www.washingtonpost.com/nation/2020/09/21
/cdc-covid-aerosols-airborne-guidelines/.
Learn about the differences between the two types of transmission, how scientists
believe coronavirus spreads, and how it affects people during the pandemic.

"Wuhan Coronavirus Kills Doctor Who Warned of Outbreak." CNN, February 8, 2020. 3:12.
    https://www.cnn.com/2020/02/08/opinions/coronavirus-bociurkiw/index.html.
    The video describes Li Wenliang's anguished warning to colleagues about a
    possible new type of coronavirus. It includes bits of live telephone interview with Li
    in his hospital bed and background scenes of life in Wuhan.

"Young Sacramento Woman Hospitalized with COVID-19: 'I Thought I Was Going to Die.'"
    Sacramento Bee, July 30, 2020. 2:22. https://www.sacbee.com/latest-news
    /article244592992.html.
    Meet Kris Obligar, the young speech therapy assistant in California who nearly died
    from COVID-19. Hear how she describes her ordeal.

INDEX

Alfonso XIII (king), 18
Anti-Mask League, 67
antiviral drugs, 87–88, 90

bacteria, 11–16, 18, 69
bats, 5, 8, 25–26, 29, 32, 35–36
Bentley, Charlotte, 51, 115
Biden, Joe, 108
blood clots, 81, 83, 86, 91
Brown-Wood, JaNay, 55
bubonic plague, 17–18, 101

case counts, 27–29, 32, 37–38, 40–41, 43, 73, 95, 97–99
Centers for Disease Control and Prevention (CDC), 20, 29, 38, 64–65, 68
climate change, 23, 119
clinical trials, 85, 88–89, 101–104
conspiracy theories, 39, 103
contact tracing, 72–73
convalescent plasma, 87
COVID-19 death rate, 32, 38, 40, 47, 69, 76, 88, 98–99
COVID-19 symptoms, 5, 15, 32, 68, 70, 75, 78–81, 83–87, 99
COVID-19 vaccine, 25, 38, 62, 84, 88–89, 97, 101–109, 116

distribution of, 101, 105–107, 109
safety of, 89, 102–104
cruise ships, 46, 48–49

distance learning, 51–53, 54–58, 116
DNA, 14, 20, 25
Doctors Without Borders, 47

Ebola, 22, 36, 47, 87, 94, 102
Ellison, Larry, 91
essential workers, 40, 44, 46, 107
evictions, 41, 46

face masks, 43, 61–68, 79–80, 84, 90, 98, 109, 111, 115–118
Fauci, Anthony, 61, 97, 102, 108, 115
flattening the curve, 61–62

Gates, Bill, 42, 103, 116

hand sanitizers, 69, 92, 112
handwashing, 61, 63, 69, 80, 109
Harton, Mia, 54–55, 116
heart damage, 80–83, 91–92
herd immunity, 108–109
HIV/AIDS, 11, 17, 19–23, 90, 94

home delivery, 114

immunity to COVID-19, 9, 23, 25, 71–72, 79, 105, 108–109, 117
influenza, 9, 11, 17–19, 23, 28, 30–32, 67, 79–80, 83–84, 101, 105, 107
Inglesby, Tom, 6
intensive care units (ICU), 66, 76, 99–100
Italy, 18, 37

Jacobsen, Amy, 54

Kirkman, Aidan, 52, 116
Kwan, Sui-chu, 26–28

Li Wenliang, 5–7, 9, 31

medications, 22–23, 27–28, 85, 87–91, 101
microbes, 5, 11, 15, 23
Middle East respiratory syndrome coronavirus (MERS-CoV), 9, 26, 30–33, 35–36, 79, 87, 102
Milano, Alyssa, 80
Moderna, 38, 104

National Institutes of Health (NIH), 101, 115
Navajo Nation, 47

obesity, 46, 76
Obligar, Kris, 66, 116, 118–119

online classes. *See* distance learning

online shopping, 114

Operation Warp Speed, 101–103

pandemic policies, 37, 39, 41, 57, 62, 68, 70–71, 95, 102, 107, 115–116

Pfizer, 38, 103–104

placebos, 89, 104

Pompeo, Mike, 8

quarantine, 5, 30, 48–49, 52, 70, 73, 83

racism, 19, 37, 44–46, 117–118

Redfield, Robert, 61, 65, 115

reopening, 41–43, 57–59, 98, 100, 112

RNA, 14, 16–17, 25

Schultze, Terry, 46, 48–49

severe acute respiratory syndrome coronavirus-1 (SARS-CoV-1), 5, 7, 9, 26–32, 35–36, 38, 79, 87, 102

social distancing, 61, 63, 68, 72, 80, 109, 112

Spanish flu, 18–19, 22, 67

stay-at-home orders, 40, 68, 117

stimulus packages, 38, 41, 101

super-spreading events, 43

T-cells, 76, 79

Tedros Adhanom Ghebreyesus, 43, 119

testing for COVID-19, 37, 43, 46, 48, 70–72, 78, 98

travel ban, 37–38

Trump, Donald, 8, 37, 39, 42, 45, 91–94, 98, 115

unemployment, 40–41, 54, 92, 100–101, 111

US Food and Drug Administration (FDA), 23, 38, 71, 87–91, 94, 103–104

ventilators, 41, 43, 75, 85, 90–91, 100

wet markets, 7–8, 26–27

working from home, 40–41, 44, 56–57, 112–114

World Health Organization (WHO), 9, 20, 28, 38, 43, 119

Wuhan, China, 5–8, 35–38, 45

Zaki, Ali Mohamed, 30–31

Zlatar, Branko, 77–78

Zuckerberg, Mark, 112

ABOUT THE AUTHOR

Connie Goldsmith has written twenty-six nonfiction books for young adult and middle-grade readers that deal with health topics, history, and military themes. She has also published more than two hundred magazine articles for adults and children. Her books include *Running on Empty: Sleeplessness in American Teens*; *Kiyo Sato: From a WWII Japanese Internment Camp to a Life of Service*; *Women in the Military: From Drill Sergeants to Fighter Pilots*; *Pandemic: How Climate, the Environment, and Superbugs Increase the Risk*; *Dogs at War: Military Canine Heroes*; and *Bombs over Bikini: the World's First Nuclear Disaster* (a Junior Library Guild Selection, a Children's Book Committee at Bank Street College Best Children's Book of the Year, and an SCBWI Crystal Kite winner). Goldsmith is a member of the Society of Children's Book Writers and Illustrators and the Authors Guild. She is a registered nurse with a bachelor of science degree in nursing and a master of public administration degree in health care. She lives near Sacramento, California.

PHOTO ACKNOWLEDGMENTS

Image credits: wonderpo99/Shutterstock.com, p. 7; AP Photo/CHINATOPIX, p. 9; Science Photo Library - STEVE GSCHMEISSNER/Getty Images, p. 12; Laura Wesltund/Independent Picture Service, pp. 13, 44, 62, 81, 86; Gil Cohen Magen/Shutterstock.com, p. 15; BSIP SA/Alamy Stock Photo, p. 17; Science History Images/Alamy Stock Photo, p. 19; AP Photo/Denis Farrell, p. 21; imageBROKER/Alamy Stock Photo, p. 21; AP Photo/Britta Pedersen/picture-alliance/dpa, p. 23; Orso/Shutterstock.com, p. 27; aaltair/Shutterstock.com, p. 29; Ole Jensen/Getty Images, p. 39; AP Photo/Michael Nigro, p. 43; zjtmath/Shutterstock.com, p. 53; insta_photos/Shutterstock.com, p. 54; insta_photos/Shutterstock.com, p. 55; Ringo Chiu/Shutterstock.com, p. 57; Fly View Productions/E+/Getty Images, p. 58; AP Photo/Michael Brochstein/Sipa USA, p. 63; AP Photo/Nancy Lane/Boston Herald, p. 65; Ekkaratk/Shutterstock.com, p. 71; Ben Thornley/Shutterstock.com, p. 73; AP Photo/Nicolò Campo, p. 77; AP Photo/Nathan Denette, p. 82; AP Photo/Alex Brandon, p. 93; Pat Greenhouse/The Boston Globe/Getty Images, p. 105; John B Hewitt/Shutterstock.com, p. 106; David Pereiras/Shutterstock.com, p. 113; VDB Photos/Shutterstock.com, p. 114; Courtesy of Kyle Obligar, p. 119.

Cover: khaleddesigner/ Shutterstock.com.